W9-ADN-120

2013

Praise for THE POWER OF ZERO

"I've always advised that taxes will be higher in the future, but was never able to articulate 'why' or deliver that message in a powerful way. McKnight's book is the most compelling case for this I've ever seen. If you're dumping money into a 401(k) or IRA, you need to read this book today."

—DAVE COX, THE PRODUCERS GROUP, BRYANT, AR

"David is a retirement visionary. His insights are clear and concise and his action plan to remove the IRS from your retirement picture is irrefutable!"

—RICK WHITE, AMERICAN PLANNING GROUP, INC., RALEIGH, NC

"The Power of Zero offers proven strategies to dampen Uncle Sam's impact on your retirement. It's a must read for those who want to take the IRS wild card out of the deck!"

—STEVE PARKER, CPA, MBA, STEVE PARKER & ASSOCIATES, LLC, ORLAND PARK, IL

"The concepts and strategies in this book have proven indispensable in getting my clients to the 0% tax bracket in retirement. Well worth the read!"

—MARK CUPP, SR., LUTCF, CUPP WEALTH STRATEGIES, SANTA CLARA, CA

"The principles in The Power of Zero have empowered me to sound the alarm and rescue my clients' financial future and security from the looming threat of higher taxes."

—JAMES "JAMIE" FARRELL, FX3 SAFE RETIREMENT PLANNING, HUNTERSVILLE, NC

"Meeting David and reading The Power of Zero has completely changed my practice and refocused my planning for my clients. Thank you, David."

—PATRICK SMITH, BERING FINANCIAL, ARLINGTON, TX

"*The strategies behind The Power of Zero have revolutionized my approach to finance, and my clients are the better for it.*"

—DAN HAWTREE, CPA, HAWTREE & ASSOCIATES, MONEE, IL

"*David's passion for designing creative solutions for his clients is unparalleled in the industry. His book provides specific insight on why it's important to reduce your income taxes and pursue the 0% tax bracket. It is a must read for financial professionals and their clients everywhere.*"

—SHAWN SIGLER, FINANCIAL INDEPENDENCE GROUP, CORNELIUS, NC

"*The Power of Zero is right on at the right time. U.S. taxes are poised to rise dramatically. The math is clear and surprisingly simple. Consumers and advisors need to know and this book tells the story.*"

—CLARK S. GARDNER, MCAP FINANCIAL GROUP, OREM, UT

"*Essential reading for anyone who wants even the slightest measure of command over their future finances. Far and away the most up to date strategies for anyone wanting to retire. Without these techniques, investors are at the mercy of circumstances beyond their control.*"

—NAVI DOWTY, CFA, NAVI DOWTY & ASSOCIATES, INC., WHEATON, IL

"*David has an incredible grasp of our country's current economic condition. The Power of Zero clearly outlines a way to introduce more certainty into my clients' financial future. Thank you Dave!*"

—WILLIAM E. SPAR, M.A., LUTCF, ADVANCED RETIREMENT PLANNING, LLC, PHOENIX, AZ

"*Like it or not, taxes are likely to rise and McKnight's proposal that we reposition our assets now so as to avoid higher taxes in the future could not be more timely.*"

—GREG GILLIS, CFP©, LITTLE ROCK, AK

"The Power of Zero is a must read for anyone who is serious about maximizing income in retirement. We use the strategies outlined in David's book daily to help our clients become as tax-efficient as possible."

—W. RAY STAGNER, CHFC, CLU, FIDLER WEALTH MANAGEMENT, TULSA, OK

"David McKnight is truly a pioneer in our industry! The Power of Zero has helped me educate and prepare my clients to reposition their taxable and tax-deferred assets to tax-free, through a balanced array of tax-free strategies."

—BRIAN HANSON, HANSON WEALTH MANAGEMENT, EDEN PRAIRIE, MN

"I have known David McKnight for many years and he is a true visionary. This book will guide retirees through the coming tax crisis by helping them take advantage of the power of the 0% tax bracket."

—TOMMY WOLFE CURRID, LUTCF, NICEVILLE, FL

"David McKnight is light years ahead of the financial planning industry. Make sure you and your advisor read this book! You owe it to yourself and your family."

—BRIAN BYARS, ADVANCED RETIREMENT PLANNING, ATLANTA, GA

"With all the economic uncertainty, The Power of Zero gives our clients a roadmap to greater predictability, control and peace of mind in retirement."

—HAL D. ALLEN, CPA, MACC, ALLRED JACKSON, NORTH LOGAN, UT

"Dave's ideas and strategies have radically redefined the way we look at retirement taxation for our clients. The Power of Zero lays out a clear and concise roadmap for anyone looking to shield their hard-earned assets from the impact of higher taxes."

—MIKE ABBOTT AND CHRIS BENNETT, ABBOTTBENNETT GROUP, CONCORD, NH

"Talking to our clients about the strategies in this book has transformed their retirement and protected them from the tax train wreck that is just around the corner."

—CHRIS HERKERT, HERKERT & ASSOCIATES, BELLINGHAM, WA

"*The Power of Zero by David McKnight offers compelling strategies to safeguard your retirement income in a future where we will likely see much higher tax rates.*"

—Donald Gladhart, CLU, ChFC, Wathena, KS

"*David has distilled the tax-efficient retirement paradigm into a single, powerful book. I've been in this business for 30 years, and this message couldn't be more timely. Thanks David!*"

—Craig Jergenson, CFP©, CoachCraig Financial, Coon Rapids, MN

"*The answer to the problem of higher tax rates is to plan for a tax-free retirement, and McKnight does a great job of laying out strategies that are available to just about anyone.*"

—Steve Smith, Pilot Financial Advisors, Salisbury, MD

"*Although my clients are well prepared for retirement, they haven't planned for the devastating effect of taxation on their Social Security. Thank you David for writing this book and raising the warning cry!*"

—Jason Redditt, Advanced Retirement Solutions, Little Rock, AR

"*David makes a very convincing argument that retirement is a lot more doable at the 0% tax bracket. The expert advice he provides on how to get there is worth the time it takes to read and implement!*"

—Earl R. Eastman, Providence Educational Institute, San Diego, CA

"*David has done a remarkable job of explaining how everyone, with just a little bit of proactive planning, can insulate themselves from the threat of higher taxes by creating a totally tax-free retirement. This is a must read for anyone interested in maximizing their wealth.*"

—Ike Ikokwu, CFP©, CPA, Atlanta, GA

THE
POWER
OF
ZERO

How to Get to the 0% Tax Bracket
and Transform Your Retirement

David McKnight

Acanthus Publishing, 2013
Boston, MA

HALF HOLLOW HILLS
COMMUNITY LIBRARY
55 Vanderbilt Parkway
Dix Hills, NY 11746

THE POWER OF ZERO:
How To Get To the Zero Percent Tax Bracket and Transform Your Retirement

Copyright © 2013, David McKnight
All rights reserved.

Printed in the United States of America

ISBN: 978-0-9890001-9-2

All rights reserved. No part of this book may be reproduced or transmitted in any form or by any means, electronic or mechanical, including photocopying, recording, or by any information storage and retrieval system, without written permission of the author, except for the inclusion of brief quotations in a review.

This publication is designed to provide accurate and authoritative information with regard to the subject matter covered. It is sold with the understanding that the publisher is not engaged in rendering legal, accounting, or other professional advice. If legal advice or other expert assistance is required, the services of a competent professional should be sought.

The information in this book is for general use and, while we believe the information is reliable and accurate, it is important to remember individual situations may be entirely different. Therefore, information should be relied upon only when coordinated with individual professional tax and/or financial advice. You need to consider your specific situation including your health and legacy goals before acting on any information presented in this book. Please note that neither the information presented nor any opinion expressed is to be considered as an offer to buy or purchase any insurance or securities products and services referenced in this book.

The information provided is not intended as tax or legal advice and may not be relied on for the purpose of avoiding any individual Federal or State tax penalties. David McKnight, his employees or representatives are not authorized to give tax or legal advice. Individuals are encouraged to seek advice from their own tax and legal counsel. They are also encouraged to seek advice from their own financial and/or insurance professional.

Published by Acanthus Publishing, Boston, Massachusetts.

COMMUNITY LIBRARY
55 Vanderbilt Parkway
Dix Hills, NY 11746

For my wife

CONTENTS

FOREWORD

by Retirement Expert Ed Slott, CPA

Taxes will be increasing. This book is a wake-up call to reality. For the past 20 years, I have been warning both consumers and advisors that the writing is on the wall and the day of reckoning is upon us. This is not a prediction but a result of plain arithmetic.

Our government will soon need huge cash infusions to meet its commitments and it will have no choice but to raise taxes on those of us who have worked hard, sacrificed, saved, and played by the rules. We were told to put money away for retirement in tax-deferred accounts like 401(k)s and IRAs, and many of us did.

Those who saved the most diligently, though, will soon realize that a substantial chunk of those tax-deferred retirement savings are sitting ducks for a revenue-hungry Uncle Sam. In fact, as your 401(k) or IRA funds grow, so does the government's share since it is a partner on your savings. But unlike a traditional business partner, Uncle Sam can increase his partnership percentage of your tax-deferred savings whenever he needs more money, and that day is coming soon.

The question is then, "Are you prepared?" You can be, but, unfortunately for most people, the answer is "no" because they believe that there is no way this can happen to them. But it can and it will. We have had federal income tax rates exceeding 90%. In fact, from 1936 to 1981, the top federal income tax rate has never gone below 70%! Higher taxes mean less money for your retirement years.

Even if you think you are prepared with a plan, it is unlikely that you are. In fact, in most cases I see, the kind of planning you need to do now to avoid the oncoming tax disaster train is not being done.

If you have to wonder if you have a plan to reduce your income taxes now and in the future, then you do not have a plan. If you don't have a plan, you will end up with what I call "The Government Plan." As you can imagine, that is not the plan that is best for you.

The plan that you need must be implemented by *you* and be done as soon as possible, before the tax train wreck arrives. You need to create a plan to move your tax-deferred funds from accounts that are forever being taxed to accounts that are never taxed. Your best defense is offense—to build tax-free savings.

The good news is that right now we are in the lowest tax rates in recent history. Now is the time to strike in order to create tax-free income for your retirement years and beyond. Even your loved ones can benefit from the planning you do now. The tax code actually includes several tax moves you can make to create tax-free retirement income but few people take advantage of them. For example, Roth IRAs and life insurance alone can help you and your family end up with more money than you have now, and with more of it tax-free.

There will never be a more cost-effective time to leverage your current assets into tax-free assets. As you move your tax-deferred funds to tax-free territory, you reduce the impact of future tax hikes on your retirement savings.

In this book, David McKnight (who, like me, also loves "tax-free"), provides you with a road map of how to get to the 0% tax bracket, virtually eliminating the tax risk, which, if not addressed, will easily consume a solid portion of your retirement savings.

It's time to face reality. Taxes will increase, and tax-deferred accounts like 401(k)s and IRAs are the low-hanging fruit waiting to be picked by Uncle Sam. Follow the steps in this book and you'll keep your hard-earned retirement savings out of Uncle Sam's reach.

I love tax-free, and you will too.

Tax-free is always better! Pay less and keep more.

—ED SLOTT, CPA
Author and Founder of *www.irahelp.com* & *www.theSLOTTreport.com*
Founder, Ed Slott's Elite IRA Advisor Group
August 12, 2013

Acknowledgements

I've had the good fortune of being mentored by some of the giants in the financial services industry over the last 16 years. It would be impossible to create a book such as this without being able to stand on the shoulders of the great people who helped make me who I am today.

One of the great mentors of my life is Dick Mack. He plucked me out of obscurity and made me believe I could amount to something great. He has a penchant for turning a phrase and, even today, I find his words and stories rolling off my tongue in everyday conversation. He is a great believer in analogies and metaphors and uses them to boil down complex concepts into simple ones. I'm still waiting for a compendium of his Dick Mack–isms to show up on the New York Times Best Seller list. He also taught me to think outside the box and find creative solutions to difficult problems. His legacy lives on through hundreds of others whose lives he continues to touch.

A special thanks also goes out to longtime colleague and mentor, Michael Minnoch, whose tax expertise helped inform a lot of my out of the box thinking on tax planning from a very early stage in my career. Michael is a true pioneer in this industry and I am proud to stand on his shoulders.

I extend my heartfelt thanks to the amazing team at Acanthus Publishing who helped with the editing, charts and layout for this book. A big thanks goes to Paige Stover for her leadership and vision throughout the entire process. My gratitude also goes out to George Kasparian and his team—David Kennedy, Ian Nichols, Morgan Rosenberg, Samantha Fahey, Andrea Weidknecht, and Timesha Livingston—who worked closely with me on the editing process and did the research behind the footnotes you see throughout the book. George and his team were kind enough to put up with my nitpicking over stylistic issues and my tendency toward compulsive and serial revising.

Finally, none of this would be possible or worthwhile without my wife, Felice. She does the heavy lifting of running our household and mothering our six amazing children. As hard as I work, I'll never work as hard as she does inside the walls of our home. Felice puts up with my long hours and road trips with grace and patience. I owe the best 13 years of my life to her unfailing companionship.

—DAVID McKNIGHT
Grafton, WI
July 31, 2013

ONE

A GATHERING STORM

"Delight in smooth-sounding platitudes, refusal to face unpleasant facts, desire for popularity and electoral success irrespective of the vital interests of the State..."

—WINSTON CHURCHILL
The Gathering Storm

On January 11, 2011, a CPA named David M. Walker appeared on national radio and made a grim prognostication: Based on the current fiscal path, future tax rates will have to double or our country could go bankrupt. He then challenged the national listening audience to come up with a four-letter word that would explain why. The calls came pouring in. "Debt?" came one answer. "Wars?" came another. "Kids?" came the next. After a few more wayward guesses, David Walker finally revealed the answer. "It's math."

Who is David Walker, and what does math have to do with the future of our country? For an 11-year period starting in 1998, David Walker served as the Comptroller General of the United States and as the head of the Government Accountability Office. In short, he was the CPA of the USA, and the nation's chief auditor. Having performed in that capacity during both the Clinton and Bush administrations, he knows more about our country's fiscal state than perhaps anyone else on the planet. Since his resignation in 2008, Walker has been crisscrossing the country, raising the warning cry, and discussing sensible solutions with anyone who will listen.

To understand the urgency behind David Walker's mission, you need look no further than the mathematical realities facing Social Security. The Social Security Act was passed into law in 1935 as the lynchpin of Roosevelt's "New Deal" with America. When it was first implemented, the math behind it (based on expected birth rates and life expectancies) ensured its financial viability into perpetuity. There were an astounding 42 workers putting money into Social Security for every one person who took money out. Ironically, the official retirement age at that time was 65, well beyond the then average life expectancy of only 62. The program's administrators didn't even anticipate that the average American would live long enough to ever draw on Social Security. If you did make it to 65, you drew on Social Security for only a few years until you died! You see,

Workers to Retiree Ratios,
Selected Years 1960 to 2060

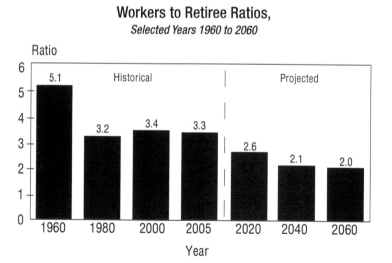

Source: Board of Trustees (2006, Table IV.B2). Projected using the intermediate assumptions in the 2006 annual report of the Board of Trustees of the Federal Old-Age and Survivors Insurance Trust Funds.

Due to a demographic glitch known as the "Baby Boomers," the workers-to-retiree ratio continues to drop, jeopardizing the solvency of Social Security and other entitlement programs.

Social Security was never intended to be a retirement program. It was merely insurance against living too long.

But then, something happened that would change Social Security forever. Soldiers came home from World War II and started to do something at a rate at which they'd never done before. They started making babies! *Great*, you may be thinking. *More babies equal more workers, which mean more contributions to the Social Security program.* That would be true if these "Baby Boomers" had decided to have nearly as many children as their parents did, but they didn't. They had 32 million fewer children. And this is where the math to which David Walker refers catches up with us.

Today, there are no longer 42 people contributing to Social Security for every one person who takes money out of the program. The ratio has fallen to 3 to 1.[1] And in another 10 years, it's going to be closer to 2 to 1. Compounding the problem, Americans can now draw Social Security as early as 62 and, due to advancements in science and medical technology, retirees are living longer than ever. The reality is, if you start drawing on Social Security at 62, you'll keep drawing it, on average, until age 85. In fact, octogenarians are the fastest-growing segment of our population!

The problem is, Social Security went from being insurance against living too long to an expensive retirement program that Americans rely upon for nearly a quarter of their lives! As of 2012, the Social Security program costs the government over $700 billion per year, or about 20% of the federal budget.[2] And the consequences for the United States couldn't be more devastating.

"A promise made is a debt unpaid"
—Robert A. Service

The math behind the Social Security problem is emblematic of a much broader crisis facing our nation. Over the years, our elected officials have

[1] "Social Security Online – HISTORY," *Social Security Administration,* http://www.ssa.gov/history/ratios.html.
[2] Fiscal year 2012 budget of the U.S. Government, Office of Management and Budget

increasingly made promises, like Social Security benefits, without any thought for how they were going to pay for them. David Walker calls these promises "unfunded obligations." The greatest of these unfunded obligations is the universal healthcare system for seniors implemented as part of Lyndon Johnson's "Great Society" domestic programs of the 1960's: Medicare. Medicare suffers from the same demographic challenges as Social Security. As of 2012, it costs the government over $500 billion per year, and these costs continue to spiral out of control. According to Walker, the fiscal strain of these two programs alone could bankrupt the United States of America.

A closer look at the numbers explains why David Walker has become so alarmed. To quantify the actual cost of these unfunded liabilities, the government employs its own unique (and creative) accounting method. Instead of telling us the actual cost of a program, they express the cost as the present value of a future obligation. For example, the government

H1 Financial Status

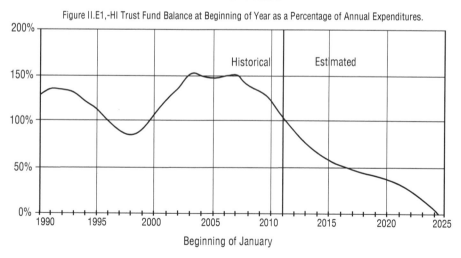

Figure II.E1,-HI Trust Fund Balance at Beginning of Year as a Percentage of Annual Expenditures.

Beginning of January

Source: Medicare Trustees Report, 2012.

According to the Medicare Trustees Report for 2012, Medicare is running a deficit and has started to dip into the trust fund accumulated over previous years. The graph above displays the Federal Hospital Insurance Trust Fund balance at the beginning of each year as a percentage of annual expenditures on the Y-axis and time in years (both historical and future) on the X-axis. These projections indicate that the trust fund will be depleted by 2025.

tells us that the cost of Social Security and Medicare is $42 trillion. What this really means is that we would have to have $42 trillion sitting in an account today, earning treasury rates, to be able to afford these programs. But the government doesn't actually have $42 trillion today, and if you look beyond 75 years, the real cost is much greater. All told, some experts put the actual cost over time at much closer to $120 trillion.

> **Present Value:** To better understand this concept, let's look at the following example. Suppose you believe that your car will need to be replaced in 10 years. You estimate that in 10 years a new car will cost you $20,000. So, you ask yourself what amount of money would have to be invested today at a reasonable rate of growth (say 5%) to be able to have $20,000 10 years from now. A quick calculation shows that $12,892 growing at 5% over that time period will give you $20,000 in 10 years' time. In other words, the present value of the future cost of your car is only $12,892!

Let's look at the math behind our country's fiscal problems from a different angle. The United States currently spends roughly 76 cents of every tax dollar it brings in on four items: Social Security, Medicare, Medicaid, and interest on the National Debt.[3] Absent any action on the

Percent of Every Tax Dollar Spent on Social Security, Medicare, Medicaid, and Interest on the National Debt

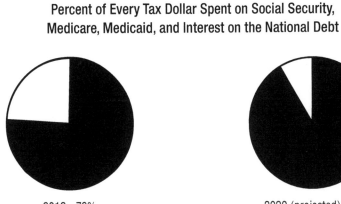

2012 - 76%   2020 (projected) - 92%

Source: Center on Budget and Policy Priorities, CNNMoney

---

[3] "Policy Basics: Where Do Our Federal Tax Dollars Go?" *Center on Budget and Policy Priorities,* last modified April 12, 2013, http://www.cbpp.org/cms/index.cfm?fa=view&id=1258.

part of Congress, however, the percentage of the government's revenue required to pay for these four big ticket items could balloon to 92 cents of every tax dollar by the year 2020.[4] As these four expenses grow and compound, they begin to crowd out all other government expenditures.

Here are just some of the programs the government would have to pay for with the remaining 8 cents: Child Nutrition Programs, Homeland Security, Food Safety and Inspection Service, U.S. Forest Service, Drug Enforcement Administration, Public Housing Program, Animal and Plant Health Inspection Service, Bureau of Indian Affairs, Army, National Endowment for the Arts, Air Force, Rural Development, Coast Guard, Supplemental Nutrition Assistance Program (aka food stamps), National Park Service, Department of Family Services, U.S. Geological Survey, Environmental Protection Agency, Centers for Disease Control and Prevention, Immigration and Customs Enforcement, Secret Service, Supportive Housing for the Elderly Program, Federal Railroad Administration, Navy, Bureau of Land Management, Peace Corps, State Department, National Science Foundation, Congress, Fish and Wildlife Service, White House, Smithsonian Institute, Small Business Administration, Federal Highway Administration, disaster relief, federal courts, federal student loans, federal pensions, income assistance, IRS, NASA, FEMA, FAA, FCC, SEC, FBI...

And the list goes on. Can you see why David Walker and a growing contingent of economists are so concerned?

But Surely Taxes Could Never Double!

The mathematical reality is that, absent any spending cuts, tax rates would *have* to double. *Come on, let's get serious*, you must be saying to yourself. *Could tax rates* really *double?*

A study of the history of taxes in the United States lends a bit of perspective. Over the last 100 years, tax rates in our country have been

---

[4] Jeanne Sahadi, "Running the government on 8¢", *CNNMoney,* January 21, 2011, http://money.cnn.com/2011/01/21/news/economy/spending_taxes_debt/index.htm.

nothing short of a rollercoaster ride. When the government first began dipping its toe in the waters of income taxation back in 1913, it seemed harmless enough. In fact, the very first federal income tax rate was only 1%. But soon the thrill of income taxation became so addicting that the government got hooked.

By the time 1943 rolled around, the highest marginal tax bracket in our country had skyrocketed to 94%. These exorbitant rates were levied on any portion of your income that exceeded $200,000.

But did anyone really make that type of money back then? Actually, there was one person with whom you may be familiar. He was an actor who later became a politician. His name was Ronald Reagan. If you look at Reagan's filmography, you'll find that he never made more than two full-length movies in a year. You see, he made about $100,000 per movie, and, for anything he made above and beyond $200,000, he only kept 6 cents on the dollar. Truth be told, he didn't even get to

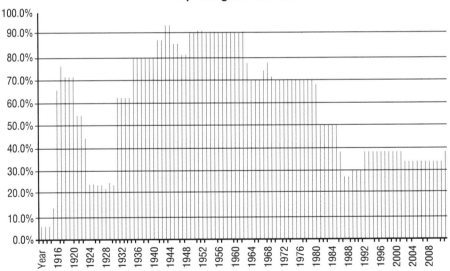

Top Marginal Tax Rates

Source: Eugene Steuerle, The Urban Institute; Joseph Pechman, Federal Tax Policy; Joint Committee on taxation, Summary of Conference Agreement on the Jobs and Growth Tax Relief Reconciliation Act of 2003, JCX-54-03, May 22, 2003; IRS Revised Tax Rate Schedules

keep that—it went off to the State of California for state tax. So, if you study the life of Reagan, you'll find that he never worked more than six months out of the year. Mathematically, it just didn't make sense.

By the '70s, things had improved, but not by much. Americans were still paying an astounding 70% on anything they made above and beyond $200,000.

Fast forward to today. The top marginal rate at which the wealthiest Americans pay taxes is a mere 39.6%. How does 39.6% stack up against some of the tax rates in the past? You could make the case that taxes haven't been this low in nearly 80 years! This is interesting because I routinely ask rooms full of people across the country, "How bad are taxes today?" And you know what they tell me? "As bad as they've ever been!" Truth is, taxes today are just about as *good* as they've ever been! The real question is, how long can these low rates last?

According to the Congressional Budget Office, if Social Security, Medicare, and Medicaid go unchanged, the rate for the lowest tax bracket would increase from 10% to 25%, the current 25% bracket would rise to 63%, and the highest bracket would go from 35% to 88%.[5]

For you skeptics out there, let me take you back in time. From 1960 to 1963, the lowest marginal tax rate was 20%, the middle bracket was 69%, and the highest marginal tax rate was an astounding 91%![6] Folks, this is a path we've been down before. What's that old adage? Those who don't study history are destined to repeat it?

A few years ago I was watching the Roadrunner with my kids. In this particular episode, Wile E. Coyote was up to his usual tactics in trying to subdue the Roadrunner. He was building a bomb—made by Acme, of course—inside a shed also made by Acme. The Coyote was so intent upon completing the bomb that he didn't realize that the Roadrunner had pushed his shed onto a train track. What's worse, he didn't realize until the very last moment that a huge freight train was bearing down on him.

[5] "Long Term Economic Effects of Some Alternative Budget Policies," Congressional Budget Office, May 19, 2008, 8–9.
[6] "Tax Foundation," *U.S. Federal Income Tax Rates*, http://taxfoundation.org/article/us-federal-individual-income-tax-rates-history-1913-2013-nominal-and-inflation-adjusted-brackets.

Now, if you found yourself on a track with a huge train bearing down on you, what would you do? You'd jump off, right? Well, when the Coyote saw the huge freight train approaching, he didn't jump out of the way. He simply pulled down the window shade, thinking that the act of doing so would make the problem go away. Did the problem go away? Of course not. There was a huge explosion and, let's face it…does the Coyote ever die? No, but as the smoke cleared, we could see the Coyote limping away from the wreckage, very much the worse for wear.

What possible application could a Roadrunner episode have to my financial life? you must surely be thinking. Well, as Americans who have grown accustomed to investing in tax-deferred accounts such as 401(k)s and IRAs, we find ourselves standing on the tracks with a very real train bearing down on us, and it's coming in the form of higher taxes. Now, given this reality, we have a couple of options. We can pretend like the problem doesn't exist and simply pull down the window shade. Or, we can implement some proven strategies that can help remove us from the train tracks.

The purpose of this book is to share with you the proven strategies that will help you get off the train tracks and insulate your money from the impact of higher taxes down the road. Which brings me to the title of this book: The Power of Zero. You see, the only real way to protect yourself from the impact of rising taxes is to adopt a strategy that puts you in the 0% tax bracket in retirement. Why is the 0% tax bracket so powerful? Because of that same four letter word: math. If you're at the 0% tax bracket and tax rates double, two times zero is still zero! By implementing these concepts before tax rates rise, you can effectively remove yourself from the train tracks and protect your hard-earned retirement savings from the gathering storm that's looming on our country's horizon.

TWO

THE TAXABLE BUCKET

G etting to the 0% tax bracket is not something that happens by accident. Enjoying a retirement free from taxation takes proactive and strategic planning, and it must begin today. The longer you wait to get off the train tracks, the less time you have to haul yourself to safety. And let's face it, taxes are not likely to stay at historical lows forever.

Critical to your journey toward the 0% tax bracket is an understanding of the three basic types of investment accounts. For our purposes, we're going to refer to these three accounts as buckets of money. The three buckets are **taxable, tax-deferred**, and **tax-free**. Contributing dollars to these accounts in a willy-nilly or haphazard way during your accumulation years can have enormous unintended consequences during your retirement years and can even prevent you from ever being in the 0% tax bracket. The goal during your working years should be to allocate the right amount of dollars to each bucket so that during retirement all your streams of income are tax-free. Defining the pros and cons of each bucket can help you understand the correct amounts to allocate to each one. This chapter will focus on the taxable bucket.

A taxable investment is one that requires you to pay taxes on the account's growth each and every year. Included in this bucket are common, everyday investments like money markets, CDs, stocks, bonds, and mutual funds.

How can you tell if your investment is taxable? The tip-off is the love letter you get from the financial institution at the end of every year. It's called a 1099. Simply put, it's a tax bill. It tells the IRS how much taxable income you earned from a given investment.

Consider the following example: If you have $100,000 in a CD and it grows 2%, you have a taxable event. You *will* have $102,000 in your account at the end of the year, but you will have to pay federal and state tax on every last bit of that 2% growth. So, $2,000 gets thrown right on top of all your other income and is taxed at your highest marginal tax rate. Assuming marginal tax rates of 30% (25% federal, 5% state), you would owe the IRS $600. So you didn't really experience $2,000 of growth, you only experienced $1,400. Thus, your after-tax rate of return on that $100,000 is only 1.4%. This annual taxation is one of the perils of the taxable bucket.

Taxable Bucket: The Ideal Balance

All this unfettered taxation, of course, raises the question, "If these investments are 100% taxable, why have them at all?" The answer is *liquidity*. Generally speaking, it's easy to get your hands on these investments, which means that they make for great emergency funds. Financial experts generally agree that we should have roughly six months' worth of income in these accounts as a buffer against life's unexpected emergencies. Having too little means that we can be forced to withdraw money from illiquid investments, incurring unwanted taxes or penalties. Having too much, on the other hand, means that we can be disproportionately affected by the rise of taxes over time. From a tax-efficiency perspective, therefore, investments in this bucket should be just the right amount: about six months' worth of income.

For example, let's say that a couple needs $4,000 per month to keep their family afloat. To determine the ideal balance in their taxable bucket, we simply take this amount and multiply it by six months. So, the most they would want to maintain in this bucket at any given time is about $24,000.

The Double Compounding Effect

Another reason to limit investment in this bucket is what I call the "double compounding effect." As your balance in the taxable bucket grows, your 1099 (or tax bill) grows as well. To make matters worse, as tax rates rise, the amount of taxes you owe on that ever-increasing 1099 likewise increases. So, in a rising tax-rate environment, your tax bill can increase at alarming rates!

Consider this example: Let's say that you make a contribution of $100,000 to a taxable investment which earns 5% per year. Because this investment is taxable, you would pay tax at your marginal rate, both state and federal. In this example, we'll use 25% federal and 5% state for a total of 30%. By the end of the first year, your pre-tax investment return is $5,000. But, when we figure in taxes at the 30% rate, your true after-tax return is only $3,500. In the chart below, we continue down this road for 10 years, raising taxes by 1% with each passing year. By the 10th year, you can see the true impact of this double compounding effect: a 74% increase in your tax bill!

Year	Combined Federal and State Tax Rate	Annual Balance	Pre-tax Investment Income at 5% Growth	After-tax Investment Income	Total Tax Bill
1	30%	$100,000	$5,000	$3,500	$1,500
2	31%	$103,500	$5,175	$3,571	$1,604
3	32%	$107,071	$5,354	$3,640	$1,713
4	33%	$110,711	$5,536	$3,709	$1,827
5	34%	$114,420	$5,721	$3,776	$1,945
6	35%	$118,196	$5,910	$3,841	$2,068
7	36%	$122,037	$6,102	$3,905	$2,197
8	37%	$125,942	$6,297	$3,967	$2,330
9	38%	$129,910	$6,495	$4,027	$2,468
10	39%	$133,937	$6,697	$4,085	$2,612

The above chart illustrates the "double compounding effect." It shows the hazards of growing and compounding an investment in a taxable environment while taxing it at ever-increasing rates.

Social Security Taxation

To further complicate matters, when you don't limit your investment in the taxable bucket, it can have unintended consequences for your Social Security benefits. In 1983, President Ronald Reagan and House Speaker Tip O'Neill helped pass a law that would tax Social Security benefits in order to ensure the long-term viability of the program.[6] Under this legislation, the IRS created income limits, or "thresholds," that determine whether or not your Social Security benefits will be taxed. The types of income that contribute to these thresholds are collectively referred to as **provisional income**. Any growth which you experience in your taxable bucket counts toward these thresholds and could potentially cause your Social Security benefits to be taxed. I will talk more about the dangers of Social Security taxation in Chapter 3.

Here's a real-life example of what can happen when you have too much money in your taxable bucket. A few years ago, an elderly couple walked into my office. When they began to describe their investments to me, one little detail knocked me clean out of my chair. They had nine CDs for $100,000 each in nine different banks. That's $900,000 in their taxable bucket! Their chief concern was their ever-increasing tax bill. I explained to them that, from a tax-efficiency perspective, they had far too much money in their taxable bucket. This huge surplus was creating unintended consequences of which they weren't even aware!

First, by having substantially more than six months' worth of income in their taxable bucket, they were exposing an unusually high percentage of their net worth to taxes. This stymied the growth of their assets and exposed them to **tax-rate risk**—the risk that taxes in the future could be much higher than they are today.

Second, by investing in a low interest-bearing vehicle, they were exposing a large portion of their assets to the eroding effects of inflation. Because their CD returns were lower than the rate of inflation, they were guaranteed to lose spending power with each passing year. Sure, some

---

[6] Matthew Dallek, "Bipartisan Reagan–O'Neill Social Security Deal in 1983 Showed It Can Be Done," *US News*, April 2, 2009, http://www.usnews.com/opinion/articles/2009/04/02/bipartisan-reagan-oneill-social-security-deal-in-1983-showed-it-can-be-done.

of that money is protected by the FDIC. But, if it's not keeping up with inflation, isn't that just going broke safely?

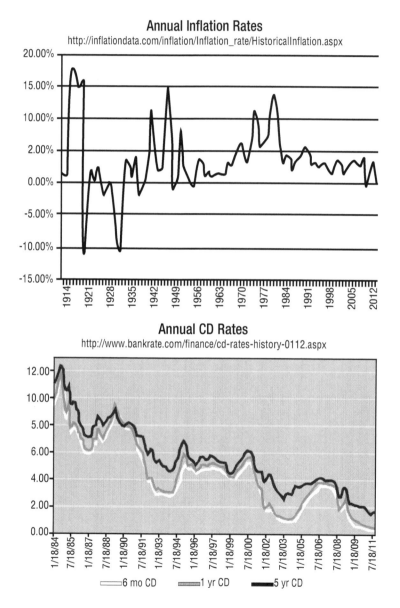

These two graphs demonstrate why investing in CDs is commonly described as the modern-day version of stashing money under the mattress. Your money may be safe and liquid, but if those funds remain invested for any substantial period of time, they are guaranteed to see a reduction in buying power due to inflation.

Third, by holding such a disproportionately large percentage of their net worth in their taxable bucket, this couple was creating a tax liability that was growing and compounding with each passing year. As tax rates climb, the real rate of return on those CDs begins to fall.

Lastly, since the pre-tax investment income from CDs is counted as provisional income, this couple was unwittingly causing their Social Security benefits to be taxed. Not only were they surrendering a portion of their investment growth to taxes, they were surrendering a portion of their Social Security as well.

Some people are tempted to put nearly unlimited amounts of money into the taxable bucket. They do so because it's liquid, it tends to be safe, and it gives them peace of mind in the event of an emergency. But all these perceived benefits come at a high cost. At the end of the day, the primary purpose of the taxable bucket is to provide a cushion against life's emergencies. That's it, nothing more. By surrendering to the impulse of having more than six months' worth of expenses in this bucket, you hinder the growth of your investments and create a laundry list of unintended consequences for your finances now and in the future. By having too much money in this bucket, you make it nearly impossible to be in the 0% tax bracket in retirement.

THREE

THE TAX-DEFERRED BUCKET

The tax-deferred bucket is likely the one with which you are most familiar. Chances are, you've been contributing to it your entire working life. If that's the case, you're not alone. The tax-deferred bucket has become the default investment account for most Americans, primarily because of the ease with which contributions are made. In the case of a 401(k) and other employer-sponsored plans, money gets zapped right out of your check and into a mutual fund portfolio. Out of sight, out of mind—what could be better? Throw in a matching contribution from your employer and it seems like a no-brainer.

However, as with your investments in the taxable bucket, there are unintended consequences of having too much money in tax-deferred accounts. In this chapter, we will explore all of the pros and cons of investing in tax-deferred accounts and we will identify the ideal balance necessary to achieve the 0% tax bracket in retirement.

The tax-deferred accounts with which Americans are most familiar are 401(k)s and Individual Retirement Accounts (more commonly known as IRAs). Other tax-deferred accounts, such as 403(b)s, 457s, SIMPLES, SEPs, and Keoghs have different rules that apply to them, but they all generally have two things in common:

1. **Contributions are tax deductible.** Generally, when you put money into this bucket, you get a tax deduction. For example, if you make $100,000 this year, and you put $10,000 into your 401(k), your new taxable income is $90,000.

2. **Distributions are treated as ordinary income.** When you divert a portion of your income to a tax-deferred investment, all you're really doing is postponing the receipt of that income until a point in time much further down the road. When you take the money out, you pay taxes at whatever the rate happens to be in the year you make the distribution. For that reason, the IRS calls these distributions ordinary income and taxes them accordingly.

When you contribute money to a tax-deferred account, it's a bit like going into a business partnership with the IRS. The problem is, every year the IRS gets to vote on what percentage of your profits they get to keep. So, you could have $1,000,000 in your IRA today, but unless you can accurately predict what tax rates are going to be in the year you make a distribution, you really have no idea how much money you have. And it's pretty hard to plan for retirement if you don't know how much money you have.

Your Tax Bracket in Retirement: Higher or Lower?

Now, some people might say, "Don't worry; it's ok to have all your retirement savings in the tax-deferred bucket because, when you retire, you'll be in a much lower income tax bracket than you were during your working years." Ever hear a financial "guru" say that? Well, it's high time we put this claim under the microscope. As we discussed in the first chapter the federal government has hugely underfunded liabilities in Social Security and Medicare programs due to changing demographics. In addition, tax rates over the past 20 years have been at historically low levels. Low tax rates and big deficits are a toxic combination that is driving our national debt to dangerously high levels. In order to liquidate all this debt, the government will have to raise more revenue.

Yet, even if we worked under the increasingly far-fetched assumption that taxes in the future are going to be the same as they are today, this much would still be true: All the deductions you experienced during your working years literally vanish into thin air right when you need them the most—in retirement.

Let's take a look at the top four deductions during a typical American's working years:

1. **Mortgage Interest:** This is far and away the number one source of deductions for those who itemize. Every year, you can deduct interest on up to $1 million of debt on your residence. But here's the problem: Most of the retirees I see week in and week out already have their home paid off. So, the biggest source of deductions is nonexistent for many retired Americans.

2. **Your Children:** This is a double whammy because your children count as an exemption and a credit. An exemption is a dollar-for-dollar reduction in your taxable income. A credit is a dollar-for-dollar reduction in your tax bill. So children, as it turns out, are a *huge* source of deductions. Are your children still living with you in retirement? You hope not, right? But even if they are, they're likely well past the age when they can be counted as dependents.

3. **Retirement Plan Contributions:** Are you still contributing to your 401(k) or IRA in retirement? Of course not! The whole reason you had these accounts was so that you could take money out in retirement, not continue to make contributions for the purpose of tax deductions.

4. **Charity:** Once charitable, always charitable. But what I've found is that, during retirement, there's less money to go around. So instead of donating money, people donate time. In lieu of making that check out to the soup kitchen, they might actually go down to the soup kitchen and ladle the soup themselves. And while this is incredibly noble and worthwhile, it simply doesn't show up on the IRS's radar. Not a deductible activity!

All of these deductions during your working years might have added up to $50,000, $60,000, or in some cases $70,000. But, absent any of these deductions in retirement, what's left? The IRS, in their infinite goodness, gives you a choice. You can add up all the above-mentioned deductions (and other miscellaneous ones) and use that total to offset your taxable income. This is known as itemizing. Or, you can take the standard deduction ($12,200), plus a personal exemption for you ($3,900) and one for your spouse ($3,900), for a total of $20,000. Because many of the itemized deductions phase out before retirement, most retirees are stuck with the standard deduction and personal exemptions.

So, if you need $100,000 per year of income in retirement and your deductions are only $20,000, then your taxable income would be $80,000 per year. That puts you at a marginal federal tax rate of 25%. Throw in another 5% (on average) for state tax, and you're looking at a marginal tax rate of 30%. That's a lot higher than most retirees are anticipating!

I can remember hearing an exchange on a financial radio show that went a little like this:

Caller:

I don't understand. I have less income in retirement than I did during my working years, yet I'm paying more in taxes. How is that possible?

Host:

Tell me about your deductions.

Caller:

Deductions? I ran out of those a long time ago

Host:
I see. I think I know your problem...

It all comes down to deductions. Even if tax rates in the future are the same as they are today, you could still end up in a higher income tax bracket in retirement than in your working years!

What Do You Truly Believe About Future Tax Rates?

Deciding whether to contribute to your tax-deferred bucket really comes down to what you think about the future of tax rates. If you think that your tax rates in the future are going to be lower than they are today, you should put as much money as you possibly can into tax-deferred investments. Get the tax deduction at today's higher rates and pay taxes at a lower rate down the road.

If, conversely, you believe that tax rates in the future will be higher, even by 1%, then mathematically you are better off limiting your contributions to this bucket. Later in this chapter, we will discuss the circumstances where contributions to the tax-deferred bucket may be a smart decision.

The Catch-22 of Tax-Deferred Retirement Plans

To further explore the pitfalls of the tax-deferred bucket, I'd like to reference Joseph Heller's *Catch-22*. The underlying theme of this famous book can help shed some light on the true nature of tax-deferred accounts.

The main protagonist in *Catch-22* is named Yossarian. He and his friends serve in bomber crews during World War II, stationed at an airbase off the coast of Italy. One by one, his friends fly into battle, get shot down, and never come back. Soon, Yossarian begins to realize that if he continues going on these bombing missions, he too will be shot down, and never come back.

So he begins to study the Air Force rules and regulations. And he comes across rule number 22. Rule 22 says that if you can successfully plead insanity, you can get honorably discharged from the Air Force. He decides that this is what he should do. So, he goes up to the Air Force physician and asks to be released from duty on the grounds of insanity. However, the physician says that the fact that Yossarian is trying to get out of flying these bombing missions is actually proof that he is perfectly sane. Therefore, he must continue to go on these bombing runs. Thus the title *Catch-22*. Do we still use the phrase "catch-22" today? You bet we do. It's like being stuck between a rock and a hard place. Darned if you do, darned if you don't. I refer to this story because any investment in the tax-deferred bucket is a perfect modern-day example of a catch-22. Here's what I mean:

The Rock: You have to remember that the IRS wants to tax you on your money so badly that, at a certain point, they will force you to take money out. This happens at age 70 ½, and it's called a Required Minimum Distribution (RMD). If you forget or choose not to take the money out, the IRS imposes what's called an excise tax. In reality it's a penalty, and it's an astounding 50% of your RMD. In other words, if you were supposed to take out $10,000 but didn't, you would get a bill in the mail for $5,000. And that doesn't even include the income tax! Throw in another 30% (25% federal and 5% state) for that, and you're looking at forfeiting 80% of whatever you were supposed to take out but didn't. As you can see, the IRS is pretty serious about getting their money.

The Hard Place: Now we understand what happens if you don't take enough money out of your tax-deferred investments. But what happens if you take out too much? Beyond paying increasingly higher amounts of tax, the IRS says that as much as 85% of your Social Security becomes taxable. *What?!* you may be thinking. *Social Security felt like a tax when it came out of my paycheck, and now they're going to tax it before I get it back? That's like a double tax!* Sadly, you read correctly.

The Bottom Line: If you take out too little, you will pay a big penalty to the IRS. If you take out more than required, you pay higher taxes on your Social Security benefits. Talk about a catch-22!

The Dirty Words of Retirement Savings: Provisional Income

As I explained in the previous chapter, Social Security benefit taxation was the result of a compromise struck between President Ronald Reagan and Speaker of the House Tip O'Neill back in 1983, when Social Security was teetering on the cusp of insolvency. Under the Reagan–O'Neill deal, up to 50% of Social Security benefits were subject to tax. At the beginning of President Bill Clinton's first term in 1993, the tax was expanded so that up to 85% of Social Security benefits became taxable, depending on income levels. [7]

Here's how it works:

As you'll recall from Chapter 2, the IRS tracks something called provisional income to determine the percentage of your Social Security that will be taxed. Anyone aspiring to the 0% tax bracket should be acutely aware of what qualifies as provisional income. The following is a list of the most common sources of provisional income:

1. One-half of your Social Security income
2. Any distributions taken out of your tax-deferred bucket (IRAs, 401(k)s, etc.)
3. Any 1099 or interest generated from your taxable bucket investments
4. Any employment income
5. Any rental income
6. Interest from municipal bonds

The IRS adds up all your provisional income and, based on that total and your marital status, determines what percentage of your Social Security benefits will become taxed. That percentage of your Social Security benefits is then taxed at your highest marginal tax rate. The provisional income thresholds are outlined below.

Joint Provisional Income for Married Couples

Provisional Income	Percent of Social Security Subject to Tax
Under $32,000	0%
$32,000 to $44,000	50%
Over $44,000	85%

[7] "Social Security: Calculation and History of Taxing Benefits," *Congressional Research Service*, January 15, 2010, http://aging.senate.gov/crs/ss24.pdf.

Individual Provisional Income for Single People

Provisional Income	Percent of Social Security Subject to Tax
Under $25,000	0%
$25,000 to $34,000	50%
Over $34,000	85%

Unfortunately, these tax thresholds are not indexed for inflation, so each year an increasing number of retirees begin to pay taxes on a portion of their Social Security benefits.

To better understand how devastating this tax can be, let's look at the example of Tom and Mary Smith. Tom and Mary have a combined $30,000 of Social Security income. They also distribute $40,000 from their IRA in an effort to meet their lifestyle needs in retirement. In order to determine their provisional income, the IRS takes half of their Social Security ($15,000) and adds it to the $40,000 that they distributed from their IRAs. So, Tom and Mary's total provisional income is $55,000. Because they're over the $44,000 threshold, 85% of their Social Security is now taxable at their highest marginal tax rate. Thus, 85% of their $30,000 of Social Security is $25,500. This amount now gets piled right on top of all their other income,

Taxation of Tom and Mary's Social Security

1/2 of Social Security Benefits:	
(1/2) x ($30,000) =	$15,000
Annual IRA distribution	$40,000
TOTAL	$55,000

Applicable % of Social Security benefits subject to tax	85%

Amount of taxable Social Security	
(85%) x ($30,000) =	$25,500
Tax rate	25%
Tax Expense	$6,375

So, how much more do we need to distribute from our IRA to replace the tax expense?

Amount needed after tax	$6,375
Marginal tax rate	30%
Additional IRA amount needed	$9,107

at which point they pay federal tax (say 25%) on $25,500, for a total of $6,375. So, Tom and Mary just paid a $6,375 tax on their Social Security, simply because they took too much money out of their IRA. Every year in which they continue to take this level of distributions from their IRA is another year they pay tax on their Social Security.

To make matters worse, Tom and Mary now have to compensate for the $6,375 which they are no longer getting from their Social Security. To do so, they will likely have to take an additional distribution from their IRA—yet another taxable event. If Tom and Mary's marginal tax rate is 30% (including 5% state tax), they'd have to take $9,107 from their IRA, just to replace the $6,375 which they lost to Social Security taxation! Wouldn't it be much simpler if Tom and Mary could get their Social Security tax-free? We will discuss how to do this in Chapter 5.

So, this is the catch-22 of traditional tax-deferred retirement accounts. Darned if you don't take enough money out (you incur a 50% penalty) and darned if you take too much out (your Social Security gets taxed).

A Math Formula That Could Sink Your IRA or 401(k)

To make matters worse, many Americans will run out of money in their 401(k)s and IRAs much faster than they think, and it's all because of a math formula that they never taught us in high school.

Let me illustrate this point by posing a math problem. Let's say that Tom and Mary need $100,000 after tax from their IRA to support their lifestyle in retirement. If Tom and Mary are at a 30% effective tax rate, how much will they have to take out of their IRA to be able to pay the tax to the IRS and still be left with $100,000 that they can then spend on their lifestyle? I've asked this question to thousands of people across the country, and you know the answer I get 90% of the time? $130,000. Now on the surface this answer makes sense. Thirty percent of $100,000 is $30,000, right? Add that to the $100,000 you need to pay for your lifestyle, and there's your answer. But is that really how it works?

It's a little bit more complex than that. If you pay 30% in taxes, then you get to keep 70%. However, 70% of $130,000 is only $91,000, which leaves you $9,000 short. To get the correct answer, you have to use a special formula. Take the amount of money you need after tax ($100,000) and divide by one minus your effective tax rate (.30). In mathematical notation, it looks like this:

$$\frac{\$100,000}{(1-.30)}$$

In essence, we're dividing 0.7 into $100,000. When we do, we get $142,857. That's $12,857 more than most Americans think. In other words, when the typical American calls up his financial advisor and says, "I need $100,000 after taxes," he thinks that his balance is going to go down by $130,000. In reality, it's going to go down by $142,857. Is it possible that quite a few Americans will be running out of money in their 401(k)s or IRAs a lot faster than they thought? It sure is, and it's all because of a simple math formula that we never learned in school.

Tax-Deferred Bucket: The Ideal Balance

So, after going to such great lengths to pooh-pooh the tax-deferred bucket, is there ever any scenario in which you *would* want to have money in these types of accounts? Let me answer that question in two parts.

First, whenever your employer is offering you free money, it's always wise to accept it. Free is good. For example, if you make $100,000 per year and your employer gives you a dollar for dollar match up to 3% of your income, contribute $3,000 but not a penny more. If your employer is willing to give you $3,000, take it! You just can't beat a 100% return on your money in that first year. As a rule of thumb, you should always put money into your 401(k) up to the employer match, but nothing more.

Some worry that by stopping contributions to their 401(k), they'll lose out on tax deductions. This is true, but you have to remember that the purpose of a retirement account is not to give you a tax deduction, it's to maximize your retirement distributions at a point in your life when you can least afford to pay the taxes—in retirement. Remember that during your working years, you generally have more deductions, more surplus cash with which to pay the tax, and (at least in the near term) historically low tax rates. In retirement, all those deductions will have been phased out, taxes will likely be substantially higher, and there will be less money to go around.

Second, there *are* legal ways to get money out of our 401(k)s and IRAs in retirement without paying any taxes at all. Let me illustrate this with an example. A 50-year-old married couple planning to retire at age 65, absent any other tax deductions, could claim *some* deductions. They would get a standard deduction ($12,200) plus a personal exemption ($3,900) for each of them for a total of $20,000. Because the IRS indexes this $20,000 to keep up with inflation (3% historically), these deductions would actually be closer to $30,000 by the time this couple retired in 15 years at age 65. That means that they could receive income from any number of taxable sources up to $30,000 without paying taxes. Now that's my idea of the perfect investment! Get a tax deduction at the outset, don't pay taxes as it grows, then take it out tax-free. You simply can't beat it!

So, how much can you have in your tax-deferred bucket without foiling your own attempts to reach the 0% tax bracket? Your tax-deferred balances need to be low enough that by the time you start to take RMDs at 70 ½, your distributions are equal to or less than your standard deductions plus personal exemptions in that year ($20,000 in 2013). Let me give you another example: John and Susan both just turned 70 ½ and have $500,000 in their IRAs. If all their other deductions have been phased out (which is likely), they could distribute from their IRAs an amount equal to their standard deductions plus personal exemptions without paying tax. Remember in 2013, all these deductions add up to $20,000.

At age 70 ½, their RMDs would be 3.65% of their $500,000 IRAs, or $18,250. Because their deductions of $20,000 are greater than their distribution ($18,250), they wouldn't owe any tax on their RMDs!

If, on the other hand, they had $1,000,000 in their IRA, their RMDs (at 3.65%) would be $36,500—far greater than their deductions of $20,000. In this case, it would be impossible for them to be in the 0% tax bracket. What's worse, that $36,500 is all provisional income and, when added to one-half of their Social Security, would exceed the $44,000 threshold. As a result, 85% of their Social Security would be taxable at their highest marginal tax bracket.

On the other hand, if they only had $100,000 in their IRA at retirement, their RMDs would be closer to $3,650. With $20,000 of claimable deductions, almost $16,350 would go unused!

While it might take a bit of math to figure out, there is generally a perfect amount to have in the tax-deferred bucket by the time you retire. In short, you want RMDs at age 70 ½ to be equal to or less than whatever your deductions happen to be in that year (which is $20,000 in today's dollars). In most cases, if you contribute only up to your employer match during working years, your 401(k) balance will be at or below this ideal amount by the time you retire.

To determine if your tax-deferred balances are already too big, you must calculate the number of years until retirement, your contributions, employer match, and the rate of growth you anticipate on your investments. If your balances are too big, you'll need to employ some of the shifting strategies we will discuss in the next chapter. A good tax-free retirement specialist armed with the appropriate software should be able to help you determine the ideal balance in this bucket today and, if necessary, identify strategies to help reposition any surplus into the tax-free bucket.

In summary, the tax-deferred bucket has a number of different pitfalls that can hinder your efforts to reach the 0% tax bracket. When used in the right amounts and under the right circumstances, however, it transforms into the perfect stream of tax-free income and makes a valuable contribution to your 0% tax strategy in retirement.

FOUR

THE TAX-FREE BUCKET

I f you're like most Americans, you have the lion's share of your wealth accumulated in the first two buckets—the taxable and the tax-deferred. If that's the case, don't despair, because there is a third bucket. Some people call this final bucket tax-advantaged, some tax-preferred, still others tax-exempt, but for our purposes, we will call it the tax-free bucket.

Now, I have to warn you, there are all sorts of investments that like to masquerade as tax-free. I'm here to tell you that to be truly tax-free, an investment has to qualify in two different ways.

First, it has to *really* be tax-free. I'm talking free from all taxes, including federal tax, state tax, and capital gains tax. We've all heard of municipal bonds, right? We've been told for years that municipal bonds are tax-free, but do they really meet the definition of a true tax-free investment? It is true that the interest from municipal bonds is free from federal tax, but it's not always free from state tax. To avoid state tax, you have to buy a bond issued by the municipality in which you live. For example, if you live in Arizona and you buy a municipal bond from California, you aren't benefiting the municipality in which you live (Arizona), so you would have to pay state taxes. How about capital gains tax? Let's say that you don't want to put all your eggs in one basket, so you buy a mutual fund of municipal bonds. Then your mutual fund increases in value and you decide to sell it. In this case, you *would* actually pay capital gains tax. So, municipal bonds don't qualify as *truly* tax-free because they can, in some circumstances, be taxed.

Second, money distributed from a truly tax-free investment cannot count as provisional income. In other words, true tax-free investments do not contribute to the thresholds that determine whether your Social Security benefits get taxed. Not to pick on municipal bonds again, but interest on these bonds does count as provisional income and may cause a portion of your Social Security to be taxed. So, an investment vehicle widely touted as tax-free doesn't even satisfy the two litmus tests required of a truly tax-free investment.

Now that we've defined a true tax-free investment, let's explore the investments vehicles that *do* qualify.

The Roth IRA

The Roth Individual Retirement Account (more commonly known as the Roth IRA) is perhaps my favorite tax-free investment because it meets both of the litmus tests I just mentioned. So long as you're at least age 59 ½, all distributions from Roth IRAs are free from federal, state, and capital gains taxes. Further, distributions from Roth IRAs do not count as provisional income and, therefore, don't cause any of your Social Security to be taxed.

Contributions to the Roth IRA are made with after-tax dollars, meaning that you do not get a tax deduction at the time of contribution. However, once your money is in a Roth IRA, your dollars grow tax-free and are tax-free upon distribution as long as you're at least 59 ½.

Now, like most good things in the financial world, the IRS does put some constraints on the Roth IRA, but this shouldn't discourage you from participating.

Contribution Limits: Any time the IRS puts limits on what you can contribute to a retirement program, your antennae should shoot up. A general rule of thumb is the more austere the limitations, the more attractive the investment vehicle. This is the case with the contribution limits imposed upon the Roth IRA. As of 2013, if you're younger than age 50, the IRS will only allow you to contribute $5,500 per year. If you're older than age 50, you have a catch-up provision that allows you to contribute $6,500 per year.[8] Compare these limits to those in traditional tax-deferred alternatives. With a 401(k), you can contribute up to $17,500 (or $23,000 if you are over age 50). With a Simplified Employee Pension (SEP), you can contribute an astounding $51,000 per year. By looking at the Roth IRA's contribution limits relative to its tax-deferred peers, we can infer that there is something valuable and compelling about this account.

Income Limits: Can Bill Gates contribute to a Roth IRA? Actually, he can't. He makes too much money. Once you approach the $178,000 income threshold for a married couple ($112,000 for singles), your ability to make Roth IRA contributions begins to phase out. How about my children, the oldest of whom is 12? Can they contribute to Roth IRAs? Nope. In order to contribute to a Roth IRA, you have to have earned income. You have to be working somewhere and earning an actual paycheck. (My kids work, I just don't pay them!) How about retirees living on Social Security and receiving distributions from their IRAs? Nope. They can't contribute to Roth IRAs because, again, they lack the earned income. Roth IRAs are designed to benefit Main Street Americans who are still earning a paycheck.

Liquidity Constraints: The IRS does allow you to access whatever you've put into your Roth IRA without penalty.[9] But to access the growth on your contributions tax-free and penalty-free, your Roth IRA account has to have been open for at least 5 years and you have to be at least 59 ½. In other words, your Roth IRA shouldn't double as an emergency fund. Any of the growth on your contributed dollars can't be accessed until age 59 ½. If money is withdrawn prematurely, additional taxes and penalties ensue. Further, once

---

[8] Emily Brandon, "401(k) and IRA Changes Coming in 2013," *U.S. News: Money*, October 29, 2012, http://money.usnews.com/money/retirement/articles/2012/10/29/401k-and-ira-changes-coming-in-2013.

[9] "Individual Retirement Arrangements (IRAs)," Department of the Treasury: Internal Revenue Service, publication 290, cat. no. 15160X, http://www.irs.gov/pub/irs-pdf/p590.pdf.

money has been withdrawn from a Roth IRA, it cannot be paid back. You will have effectively forfeited your ability to grow the money you distributed on a tax-free basis for the rest of your life. Once you make a distribution, you lose those tax-free dollars, along with all future growth.

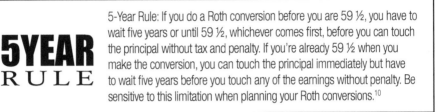

5-Year Rule: If you do a Roth conversion before you are 59 ½, you have to wait five years or until 59 ½, whichever comes first, before you can touch the principal without tax and penalty. If you're already 59 ½ when you make the conversion, you can touch the principal immediately but have to wait five years before you touch any of the earnings without penalty. Be sensitive to this limitation when planning your Roth conversions.[10]

Constraints on Roth IRA Contributions and Liquidity

Filing Status	Adjusted Gross Income	Contribution Limits	Liquidity
Married, filing jointly	Less than $178,000 before phase out starts	Younger than 50: $5,500 per year Older than 50: $6,500 per year	Contributed Funds: Available for withdrawals at any time without penalty Funds from Growth: Subject to taxes/penalties on withdrawals prior to age 59$^{1/2}$
Single	Less than $112,000 before phase out starts	Younger than 50: $5,500 per year Older than 50: $6,500 per year	Contributed Funds: Available for withdrawals at any time without penalty Funds from Growth: Subject to taxes/penalties on withdrawals to age 59$^{1/2}$

To reiterate, just because Roth IRAs have constraints doesn't mean you shouldn't contribute to them. In fact, I would say that because they have constraints you *should* be contributing to them. Remember, Congress and the IRS only let you have so much of a good thing.

The Math and Science behind Roth IRA Contributions

In what circumstances should you contribute to a Roth IRA? The answer depends on whether or not you will be in a higher or lower tax bracket when you take the money out in retirement. That's it. End of story.

---

[10] Kelly Green, "Nuts and Bolts of Five-Year Rule on Roth IRAs," The Wall Street Journal, November 7, 2009, http://online.wsj.com/article/SB125754645803734655.html.

You may have heard the argument that Roth IRAs are deficient because you're contributing after-tax dollars. This argument suggests that since you are contributing after-tax dollars, you aren't able to contribute as much and, therefore, won't have as much money over the long-term. Let's use a little bit of math to debunk this financial myth. Again, the only determining factor in whether you should contribute to a Roth IRA is what you think your tax rate will be when you retire. Let me illustrate with the example of twin brothers Gary and Doug, age 35.

Gary is in a 30% tax bracket and likes the idea of tax deductions, so he opts for the tax-deferred approach. He decides to put $5,000 of pre-tax dollars into his 401(k) each year with no match from his employer. He then lets it grow and compound at 8% for the next 30 years. By the time he retires at age 65, he has $611,729 in his 401(k). Only, he doesn't really have that much because he hasn't paid taxes yet. Remember, the only dollars that really matter are those which we can spend after tax, right? Let's also assume that tax rates when Gary is 65 (suspending disbelief for just a moment) are still at 30%. How much of that $611,729 is left after tax, assuming that he pays 30% tax on all distributions? The answer is $428,211.

Gary's brother Doug opts for the tax-free approach with his Roth IRA. Because he's contributing dollars that have already been taxed at 30%, he can now only invest $3,500 per year. He grows these dollars over the same period of time, and then decides to retire at age 65. How much money will he have? Would you be surprised if I told you $428,211? It's the same as Gary, down to the last red penny!

What's the moral of the story? If tax rates in the future are the same as they are today, it doesn't matter which IRA you choose, Roth or traditional. However, if tax rates in the future are just one percent higher, you're better off choosing the Roth IRA. In Gary's case, 1% higher taxes means he's left with only $422,093, in which case Doug wins!

In order to determine whether you should put your money into a tax-deferred or tax-free investment, you have to ask yourself what you truly believe about the future of tax rates. If you think that tax rates in the future will be higher than they are today, then you should invest in tax-free accounts. If you think tax rates in the future will be the same as today, then it doesn't really matter. If, in the unlikely event, you think tax rates in the future are going to be lower than today, then you should put money hand-over-fist into your tax-deferred account.

401(k) vs. Roth IRA
Ending Balances with Same Tax Rate and Higher Future Rate

	No Change in Tax Rate		1% Increase in Tax Rate	
	Gary	Doug	Gary	Doug
Vehicle	401(k)	Roth IRA	401(k)	Roth IRA
Contribution Per Year	$5,000	$5,000	$5,000	$5,000
Tax Rate at Age 35	30%	30%	30%	30%
After-Tax Contribution Per Year	$5,000	$3,500	$5,000	$3,500
Average Rate of Return Per Year for 30 Years	8%	8%	8%	8%
End Value of Investment at Age 65	$611,729	$428,211	$611,729	$428,211
Tax Rate at Age 65	30%	30%	31%	31%
After-Tax End Value	$428,211	$428,211	$422,093	$428,211

So, as you read the headlines and take inventory of our country's fiscal condition, ask yourself where tax rates are going to be when you retire. Factor in the reality that you will have very few deductions in retirement, and then make your decision accordingly. If you have even the slightest notion that tax rates could be higher, then you'll have more money to spend in retirement if you invest in a Roth IRA.

Nondeductible IRA: Becoming a Convert

If you have income that exceeds the income thresholds and have been phased out of Roth IRA contributions, there are alternatives. One such alternative is the nondeductible IRA.[11]

With nondeductible IRAs, you contribute to the tax-deferred bucket, only with after-tax dollars. Once you've made these contributions, you can then convert them to a Roth IRA. Because you're contributing dollars that have already been taxed, there are no tax consequences upon conversion to a Roth IRA. If you decide to wait until the end of the year before you convert, there may be some taxable gain if the investment grows, but because you've already paid taxes on the contributions, the tax you would pay would likely be nominal.

In short, you start out making contributions to the tax-deferred bucket, but upon conversion it ends up in the tax-free bucket. It just requires signing one extra piece of paper—a conversion request.

Limitations: Once again, any time the IRS leaves an opening like this, you can be sure there are going to be restrictions. Here's the caveat: even though you're contributing after-tax dollars to your nondeductible IRA, you may still owe tax upon conversion if you have pre-tax contributions and gains in other non-Roth IRA accounts.[12]

Here's how it works: let's say that you contribute $5,500 to a nondeductible IRA and then decide to convert it to a Roth IRA. Let's also say that you have $200,000 in a traditional IRA. To calculate the tax implications on your conversion you must add the $5,500 to your existing $200,000 IRA and then divide the pre-tax amount by the total IRA balance. When you divide $200,000 by $205,500, you get 97%. This is the portion of your nondeductible IRA balance that would be taxed upon conversion. So, 97% of $5,500 ($5,335) will now be taxed at your highest marginal tax bracket. At the 30% rate (25% Federal and 5% State), you would owe $1,650 of tax on a nondeductible IRA balance you already

11 "Individual Retirement Arrangements," *IRS.gov*, http://www.irs.gov/pub/irs-pdf/p590.pdf.

12 William Perez, "The Tax Cost of Converting to a Roth," *About.com*, March 19, 2012, http://taxes.about.com/od/retirementtaxes/a/Roth-IRA-Conversions_2.htm.

paid taxes on! Paying more tax than necessary, of course, runs counter to everything this book hopes to accomplish.

Now, you could have $200,000 in a 401(k), 403(b) or even a 457, and this rule would not impact you. In that case, you could convert your nondeductible IRAs all day long with little, if any, tax liability. But if you have any money at all in a traditional IRA, you may want to think twice before adopting this tax-free strategy.

Roth Conversions: Ditching the Traditional IRA

In the right circumstances, converting from a traditional IRA to a Roth can be a very useful and efficient way to shift dollars into the tax-free bucket. By paying taxes today, you can take advantage of historically low rates while they're still around. If you still have plenty of deductions, these could help offset the taxes. Lastly, if you're at the apex of your earning years, you may have plenty of surplus capital with which to pay those taxes.

Roth conversions, however, cannot be undertaken haphazardly. In most cases, the timing has to be just right. Here's an example. Let's say that you're age 50 and have $500,000 in your traditional IRA. Let's also say that you're anxious to convert this IRA to a Roth before a precipitous rise in tax rates. So, you decide to convert all $500,000 in one year. Just to make our math easy, let's assume your tax rate on this conversion is 40% (35% federal, 5% state). You'd owe the IRS $200,000, right? Well, here's the problem. Do you have $200,000 just lying around that you would love to send to the IRS? Probably not. Some might suggest that you pay the $200,000 tax bill right out of the IRA itself. If you went this route, however, you would incur a 10% penalty for early withdrawal. That's a $20,000 mistake! Unless you have piles of money languishing in your taxable bucket earmarked for taxes, you may want to postpone conversion until you're at least 59 ½.

How Much Should I Convert?

As discussed earlier, it may be advantageous to leave some money in your tax-deferred bucket. Remember, you will still have your standard deductions and personal exemptions in retirement. These will help you offset the distributions coming out of your tax-deferred account. If you have shifted all your IRAs to the tax-free bucket, you won't be able to utilize your standard deductions and personal exemptions. That means that you may have needlessly paid a tax in order to reposition these assets. You should strive to have an IRA balance large enough so that RMDs at 70 ½ are equal to these standard deductions and personal exemptions.

Once you have determined the perfect amount of money to have in your IRA, you can then go about converting the rest of your tax-deferred assets. As a reminder, if you convert the money too quickly, that may bump you up into a higher tax rate, forcing you to pay more taxes than intended. If, on the other hand, you convert your money too slowly, you might not get all the heavy lifting done before tax rates really start to sky-rocket. A good tax-free retirement specialist can lay out a strategy that will allow you to convert the right amounts of money, at the right time, while paying as little tax as possible.

FIVE

THE LIRP

N otwithstanding your best efforts to reposition assets into tax-free accounts by traditional means, sometimes it's just not enough. The tax-free alternatives that we've discussed up to this point have constraints and may only have limited impact on your efforts to get to the 0% tax bracket. To compensate for these limitations, it may be necessary to avail yourself of another tool in your efforts to achieve a tax-free retirement: the Life Insurance Retirement Plan (LIRP). The LIRP is an accumulation tool that shares many of the tax-free attributes of traditional retirement accounts such as the Roth IRA. Not only are distributions truly tax-free, but they also don't contribute to the provisional income thresholds that trigger the taxation of Social Security benefits. The LIRP has additional characteristics that make it a surprisingly effective tool in helping you reach the 0% tax bracket in retirement.

A LIRP is essentially a life insurance policy that is specifically designed to maximize the accumulation of cash within the policy's growth account. It accomplishes this by turning the traditional approach to life insurance on its ear. Conventional wisdom says that when purchasing life insurance, you should purchase as much insurance as you can for as little money as necessary. With a LIRP, you are buying as little insurance as is required by the IRS while stuffing as much money into it as the IRS allows. When utilized as a tax-free accumulation tool, the LIRP has a number of surprising benefits.

No Contribution Limits

As mentioned in the previous chapter, contributions to the Roth IRA are capped. If you're younger than age 50, you can contribute as much as $5,500 per year (as of 2013). Once you turn 50, you can contribute up to $6,500 per year. If you find yourself in the position where your asset re-position strategy requires a shift that exceeds the allowable contributions to the Roth IRA, the LIRP can be very useful. The IRS poses no limitations on the amount of money that you can annually contribute. They only stipulate that the amount of your contributions be tied to a specific death benefit amount. Again, the key is to buy as little life insurance as is required by the IRS while maximizing contributions.

No Income Limits

If you find yourself hamstrung by the income limitations imposed by the Roth IRA and discover that your traditional IRAs make the nondeductible IRA option infeasible, the LIRP may be an attractive alternative. This is because the IRS poses no income limitations on LIRP contributions. It should come as no surprise, then, that about 85% of the CEOs of Fortune 500 companies utilize the LIRP as one of their primary retirement tools. In short, if you earn too much money or lack the necessary earned income to contribute to a Roth IRA (e.g., you're retired), the LIRP can be a powerful alternative.

No Legislative Risk

Because tax-free accounts cost the government billions of dollars per year, they are an ever-growing target for revenue-hungry legislators. However, if history serves as a model, the LIRP will likely be immune from the impact of tax-law changes. When Congress changed the rules on LIRPs in 1982, 1984, and 1988, existing LIRP arrangements continued to be taxed under the old laws. In 2005, President Bush convened the President's Advisory Panel on Federal Tax Reform in order to iron out the many inconsistencies and "loopholes" in the Federal Tax Code.[13] At that time, LIRPs came under intense scrutiny. Here is an excerpt from Chapter 6 of the panel's report:

> *Some life insurance policies...allow for nearly unlimited tax-free savings... Under the Simplified Income Tax Plan, the increase in value in those policies would be treated as current income, and therefore would be subject to tax on an annual basis, just like a savings account.*

At first glance, it seems like the death knell for LIRPs, right? A few paragraphs later, however, we get the grandfather clause:

> *Annuities, life insurance arrangements, and deferred compensation plans that currently are in existence would continue to be taxed under current-law rules.*

Although the panel's tax reform recommendations were never adopted, the above excerpt shows that there is a good chance that LIRPs already in place would survive similar legislative efforts in the future. Such grandfather clauses give the LIRP a much longer shelf life than traditional tax-free alternatives.

For example, if Congress were to act on legislation to eliminate the Roth IRA, you would likely be able to keep the money currently in your Roth IRA, but you would lose the ability to make further contributions. In contrast, the grandfather clauses that have historically affected the LIRP preserve the cash within the LIRP growth account and protect the ability to make ongoing contributions over the life of the program. This

---

[13] "Final Report – November 1, 2005," *TaxReformPanel.gov*, November 6, 2005, http://govinfo.library.unt.edu/taxreform-panel/final-report/index.html.

can be a very powerful way to protect your ability to contribute dollars to a tax-free account, regardless of congressional legislation.

Multiple Accumulation Strategies

In addition to its tax-free benefits, the LIRP provides a compelling array of options for growing dollars within the tax-free accumulation account. You are free to choose between one of three basic accumulation strategies at the outset of the program. Determining the right one for you will depend on your individual goals and objectives.

1. Insurance Company Investment Portfolio: You can opt to grow your money within the general investment portfolio of the insurance company that administers the program. Because insurance companies are in the business of managing risk, these types of returns tend to be conservative, but very consistent.

2. Stock Market: You can pass your contributions through insurance companies into mutual fund portfolios called sub-accounts. While this approach can provide much higher returns, it does expose you to the impact of severe market declines. Many Americans have steered clear of this approach in the wake of the economic collapse of 2008.

3. Index: You can contribute dollars to an accumulation account whose growth is linked to the upward movement of a stock market index like the S&P 500. You can participate in the growth of this index up to a cap, typically between 13% and 15%. On the flip side, if the index ever loses money, the account is credited zero, so that it never actually goes down in value. With back-tested historical returns between 7% and 9%, this can be a safe, but productive way to accumulate tax-free dollars for retirement.

A Balanced Approach to Tax-Free Investing

To many, the LIRP sounds like the perfect tax-free retirement tool. "Why not put all our money into the LIRP?" some might ask. For starters, it's never a good idea to have all your eggs in one basket. Not only should you diversify your investments, you should also diversify your sources of tax-free income. Also, you have to remember that the LIRP is a life insurance policy. The IRS stipulates that, in exchange for nearly unlimited tax-free savings, you must be willing to pay for the cost of term life insurance out of your accumulation account on a monthly basis. Now, if you've already budgeted for the cost of term life insurance, it may make sense to recapture those premiums, divert them to the LIRP, and then take advantage of a huge bucket of tax-free dollars that wasn't previously available to you.

In some cases, however, life insurance may not be at the top of your list. Perhaps your children have moved out and your house is paid off. Maybe your retirement accounts have accumulated to the point where you feel "self-insured." The companies that sponsor LIRPs understand this and, in some cases, have done something to sweeten the pot.

Life Insurance as Long-Term Care: Doing Double Duty

Some life insurance companies offer a provision whereby clients can access death-benefit proceeds prior to death for the purpose of paying for long-term care. This is a compelling alternative to traditional long-term care insurance policies where clients pay premiums for protection which they hope to never use. When clients utilize the LIRP to cover long-term care risks, they still pay for it, but if they die never having needed it, their heirs still receive a tax-free death benefit.

At this point you may be thinking, *that's all well and good, but do I really need long-term care?* Actually, long-term care is showing up on more and more people's radars due to the impact that a long-term care event can have on a couple's lifestyle in retirement. This may sound callous, but in some cases you're actually better off financially to have a spouse die than to go into a nursing home. Let me illustrate with an example:

Let's say that Mike Edwards has a $500,000 IRA, a pension that brings in $20,000 per year, and Social Security benefits that bring in $15,000 per year. His wife, Susan, was a stay-at-home mom and did the noble work of raising the children. As a result, she never got the chance to contribute to a retirement program. Mike reaches age 65 and has a stroke. He can no longer feed or transport himself and needs long-term care in a nursing home. Before Medicaid (the government's medical assistance program) steps in to pay the bill, they will require Mike and Susan to go into "spend down". This means that all the qualified assets in Mike's name (in this case, his IRA) will have to be diverted to the long-term care facility to offset the cost of care. Further, a portion of the pension and Social Security benefits in Mike's name will likewise be earmarked for the long-term care facility. Any jointly held assets will have to be spent down to $115,920 before Medicaid steps in to pay the bills.[14]

After her husband's stroke and transfer to a long-term care facility, Susan becomes what is called a "community spouse." As such, Susan's retirement accounts are protected from spend down.[15] The problem is, Susan doesn't have any retirement accounts. You see, she was relying upon Mike's IRA, pension, and Social Security benefits to support her in retirement.

Now let's turn the tables. If Mike were to die, Susan would simply become the beneficiary of his pension, Social Security benefits, and $500,000 IRA. From a financial perspective, Mike's death, while tragic, wouldn't turn Susan's financial world upside-down.

However, because Mike's stroke necessitates long-term care, most of his assets risk being diverted to the long-term care facility. All that Susan gets to keep is one house, one car, the $115,920 of cash, and a Minimum Monthly Maintenance Needs Allowance (MMMNA).[16] Somehow I don't think this is the type of retirement she was hoping for.

You can see how the absence of long-term care coverage can really upset one's financial apple cart in retirement. The problem is, the traditional solution—long-term care insurance—can be costly and onerous.

---

[14] Medicaid is a federally funded program that is administered on the state level. As such, each state has different rules governing Medicaid eligibility, Community Spouse Resource Allowances (CSRE), "countable asset" exemptions, etc.

[15] This exemption from spend down for the community spouse's qualified plans varies from state to state. Check the applicable laws in your state for further guidance.

[16] The MMMNA varies from state to state.

What's worse is you could pay those premiums for 20 years and then die peacefully in your sleep never having needed them and they won't send you your money back.

In the case of the LIRP, your death benefit doubles as long-term care insurance. In the event that you do die peacefully in your sleep 20 years from now, never having needed long-term care, someone still gets a death benefit. So, there isn't this feeling that you're paying for something you hope you never have to use.

The True Costs of a LIRP

Because the LIRP can seem novel or unfamiliar, many thoughtful and proactive investors are researching it before incorporating it into a well-balanced, tax-free approach to retirement. In the course of their research, clients are invariably drawn to third-party critiques on the internet offered by independent "financial gurus." Curious about what was being written by these online opinion makers, I decided to make my own foray into cyberspace.

To my surprise, I found online assessments of the LIRP to be somewhat negative and largely uniform. In fact, if I could sum up the majority of their misgivings in one statement, it would be: "LIRPs have high fees!"

Do LIRPs *really* have high fees? If so, compared to what? To establish a baseline, I decided to look at the average fees for America's most popular retirement account: the 401(k). According to *USA Today*, the total expenses for a typical 401(k) plan are about 1.5% of the entire account balance per year.[17] These fees go to pay record keepers, financial advisors, and mutual fund managers. In practical terms, this means that if your account's growth were 8.5% in a given year, your statement would show a net growth of only 7%.

Now that we have a baseline, we can see how the average fees in a LIRP stack up by comparison. Generally speaking, the fees in a LIRP

---

[17] David Pitt, "Shining a Light on 401(k) Fee Reports in 2012," *USA Today: Money*, http://usatoday30.usatoday.com/money/perfi/retirement/story/2011-12-30/401-k-disclosures-to-increase/52294254/1.

are higher in the early years and lower in the later years. Considered over the life of the program, however, these fees can average as little as 1.5%.[18]

Like I mentioned earlier, the key to attaining this low-level of expense lies in the proper structuring of the LIRP contract from the outset. To maximize cash accumulation and minimize expense, the contract must contain as little life insurance as possible while being funded at the highest level allowed under IRS guidelines. This "maximum-funding" scenario ensures that the level of expenses, as a percentage of the overall contributions, remains as low as possible.

The Economics of an ATM Machine

The best way to understand a properly structured LIRP contract is to consider an ATM machine. Whether you withdraw $20 or $200 from the ATM, your fee will always be roughly $2.50. If the fee never increases, then the very best value is to withdraw as much cash as the ATM machine allows. In a way, the same can be said of a LIRP. Whether you contribute the minimum required to keep the policy in force or the maximum allowed under IRS guidelines, your expenses won't change. To achieve fees as low as 1.5% over time, the death benefit must be reduced as low as possible while at the same time maximizing contributions.

The expenses you do pay, as I mentioned, go toward the cost of life insurance. So you are paying fees, but you're getting something valuable in return: A tax-free life insurance death benefit when you die or a long-term care benefit during your lifetime. The moral of the story is this: Whatever road you take with your retirement accounts, someone's going to be making roughly 1.5%. The question is, what are you getting in exchange for that 1.5%?

To focus solely upon the fees inside the LIRP, however, is to miss the broader picture. The real question that every potential LIRP owner should ask himself is, "Do the benefits of owning a LIRP outweigh the

---

[18] David McKnight, "Equity Indexed Universal Life – The Rest of the Story," *Signature Financial Group*, January 5, 2012, http://www.signatureadvise.com/2012/01/05/equity-indexed-universal-life.

costs inherent to the investment?" Once again, a qualified tax-free retirement specialist can help you quantify the exact benefits of implementing a LIRP. If the math demonstrates that the LIRP can push you further ahead than where you would otherwise be, then it could be a welcome compliment to your other tax-free streams of income in retirement.

"Why Haven't I Heard of a LIRP?"

Historically, the LIRP has been reserved for the wealthy segment of America's population. As already mentioned, about 85% of the CEOs of Fortune 500 companies utilize LIRPs, as do quite a few members of Congress. In the past, LIRPs were weighed down by large expenses and provisions that made distributions difficult and costly. It was a great way to pass money tax-free to the next generation, but it was an inefficient retirement tool.

It wasn't until recently that companies began to re-engineer these programs to mimic the Roth IRA. They knew that if they could structure the LIRP to capture the tax-free qualities of the Roth IRA in a low-cost way, they would benefit the everyday investor.

Tax-Free Bucket: The Ideal Balance

Now that we know that the LIRP and other tax-free alternatives exist, how much should you allocate to the tax-free bucket? To understand this, it's useful to review the ideal balances for both the taxable and tax-deferred buckets. The taxable bucket should have roughly six months of income to protect against life's unexpected emergencies. The balance in the tax-deferred bucket should be low enough that RMDs at age 70 ½ are equal to or less than your standard deductions plus personal exemptions for that year. Any dollar amount above and beyond the ideal balance in these first two buckets should be shifted to tax-free.

Any contributions that are currently earmarked for the first two buckets need to be re-evaluated according to the guidelines discussed in the previous chapters. For example, if you already have six months' worth of income in your taxable bucket yet you're still making contributions on a monthly basis, you should re-direct those dollars to the tax-free bucket. Likewise, if you're making contributions to your 401(k) above and beyond the match, these surplus dollars should be diverted to the tax-free bucket. Roth IRAs and LIRPs can be useful investment tools for doing so.

Remember, if your goal is to be in the 0% tax bracket in retirement, it's critical that you have the ideal amount of assets in each of the three buckets. If you contribute to any of these buckets in a haphazard way, you might unwittingly disqualify yourself from being in the 0% tax bracket. As a result, you expose yourself to tax-rate risk, which could ruin your dreams of a tax-friendly retirement. Again, a tax-free retirement specialist can help you analyze your first two buckets and make recommendations for shifting assets to your tax-free bucket.

SIX

Putting It All Together

A CASE STUDY

S o far, we have presented mounting evidence that points toward the need for higher taxes in the near future. We have also suggested that the best way to insulate yourself from the impact of these rising tax rates is to put yourself in the 0% tax bracket. Remember—if tax rates double, two times zero is still zero! We've also identified the pros and cons of the three basic types of investment accounts and the ideal amount of assets to have in each.

To give some real life application to everything we've discussed thus far, let's take a look at a case study involving Bob and Sue Jones.

Before we go on, please note that the Jones's situation is likely different than your own. In fact, there may even be massive disparities between your financial situation and theirs. But that doesn't make this chapter any less relevant to you. Regardless of your financial position, there is certain to be something in this example that has very real application to your retirement planning. Having said that, let's dive in.

Bob and Sue's financial profile is as follows:

The Jones's Financial Profile	
General Information	
Bob Jones's Age	50 years
Sue Jones's Age	50 years
Retirement Age	65 years
Joint Income	$100,000
Assets	
IRA Accounts	$500,000
Taxable Mutual Funds	$100,000
401(k)	Contributing 10% of income, no matching contribution from employer
Insurance	
Life Insurance	Each has a term life insurance policy lasting 20 years with a death benefit of $500,000; total premium is $2,000 per year
Long-Term Care Insurance	$4,000 per year, joint coverage

Before we dig into the Jones's situation, you should know that I've trained thousands of financial advisors on the tax-free retirement planning process. In doing so, I've sat in on their client meetings and listened to them as they talked to clients just like Bob and Sue. Because of this experience, I can tell you exactly how an initial conversation might go in the "traditional" world of financial planning. It might sound a bit like this:

> "Mr. and Mrs. Jones, I have to applaud you. You have $500,000 in your collective IRAs. Congratulations! You've done a great job saving for retirement. There's only one problem. Last year when you were down the road at XYZ Company, you only earned 7% on these IRAs. We think we can get you 8%. So, roll all your money over to us."

Sound familiar? It gets better:

> "As far as the $100,000 in your mutual funds goes, that's a great emergency fund. Problem is, last year you only got 4%. We think we can get you 5% so let us manage that for you as well. As for your 401(k) with no match, keep on doing it. When you switch jobs, give me a call. We'll roll your 401(k) into your IRA and get everything under one roof, maybe save you some fees. As for your term insurance and long-term care—well, it's not really what we do, but who are we to say you shouldn't keep doing it?"

Over the years, I've heard this conversation time and time again. There are a couple of problems with this type of approach. First and foremost, all the emphasis is on rates of return. "You're getting x. I think I can get you x+1." Second, this approach takes no thought for the types of accounts within which that growth is taking place. By letting these accounts grow in an unbridled way, you unleash a storm of unintended consequences during retirement, the most severe of which is the reality that you may never be in the 0% tax bracket.

To understand the other potential pitfalls, let's address these accounts one at a time.

Traditional IRAs: $500,000

I'm not so much concerned with what's in Bob and Sue's IRAs today as what their IRAs will be worth 15 years from now when they retire at age 65. If these IRAs grow at 8% annually over that time span, they'll have a little over $1.5 million by retirement time. "What's the problem?" you may be saying. "Who wouldn't want to have that type of balance in their IRA at retirement?"

The problem is taxes. In fact, the RMDs alone on $1.5 million would put Mr. and Mrs. Jones in one of the highest marginal tax brackets. At that point, the IRS has them exactly where they want them, and there's very little Bob and Sue can do about it. What's worse, because their RMDs are greater than their standard deductions and personal exemptions, it would be impossible for them to be at the 0% tax bracket. Instead, they would be exposed to the whims of the IRS.

To make matters even worse, because their entire RMD is counted as provisional income, 85% of their Social Security would be taxed at their highest marginal tax bracket. As a result, Bob and Sue will have to take even higher distributions out of their tax-deferred bucket to compensate. This, in turn, accelerates the rate at which they spend down their retirement assets.

What's the solution? Bob and Sue must bridle the growth of their IRAs. We want to prevent these IRAs from ever getting to $1.5 million. Notice, I didn't say that we don't want Bob and Sue's money to grow. We do want it to grow, just not in that type of account. In order to bridle the growth of this money, they must reposition a portion of it into the tax-free bucket.

A popular solution that people often discuss in this situation is the traditional IRA to Roth IRA conversion (commonly known as a Roth conversion). Roth conversions can be very powerful shifting tools, but not necessarily when you're 50 years old. In order to convert that $500,000 IRA, Bob and Sue would have to pay taxes. To make our math easy, let's assume a tax rate of 40%. Like we discussed in Chapter 4, many 50-year-olds don't have $200,000 just lying around earmarked to pay taxes.

Once again, if they pay that $200,000 tax out of the IRA itself, it is counted as a premature distribution and incurs a 10% penalty.[19] Because of this, I wouldn't recommend that Bob and Sue do a Roth conversion prior to 59 ½. They simply don't have the liquid cash to pull it off.

So how can Bob and Sue get money out of their IRAs pre-59 ½ without paying a penalty? They would have to avail themselves of a little-known section of the IRS tax code: 72(t). Section 72(t) allows you to take

---

[19] "Retirement Plans FAQ regarding Substantially Equal Periodic Payments," *IRS*, March 5, 2013, http://www.irs.gov/Retirement-Plans/Retirement-Plans-FAQs-regarding-Substantially-Equal-Periodic-Payments.

As stipulated by the IRS, funds contributed to investment vehicles such as IRAs or non-qualified annuities are locked into the investment until the money "matures." Money in these accounts typically matures when the investor turns 59½. Any and all funds taken out of these accounts prior to their maturity date are subject to 10% prematurity fees in addition to any income tax incurred by the withdrawal. Section 72(t) essentially allows investors to forgo the 10% fee by making SEPPs, or a series of substantially equal periodic payments.

Source: "72(t) 72(q) SEPP Introduction," 72 on the Net, http://www.72t.net/72t/Introduction.

substantially equal periodic payments (SEPP) on an annual basis before age 59 ½ without paying a penalty.[20] According to the IRS, you need to take money out for 5 years or until 59 ½, whichever is longer. In the case of Mr. and Mrs. Jones, they would have to take money out for 9 ½ years, or until 59 ½.

This shouldn't be a sticking point because they're already convinced that they need to suppress the growth of this account through asset shifting. Shifting these dollars over 9 ½ years spreads the tax liability over a longer period of time.

The Case for Paying Taxes Today

Paying taxes on IRAs before the IRS requires you to pay them is a leap of faith for a lot of folks. It just seems so counterintuitive. Why not postpone the payment of those taxes until the IRS forces you to pay them later on in life? When faced with this impulse, you have to crowd emotion out of the decision. There are three very good mathematical reasons for paying those taxes today:

1. **Historically Low Tax Rates**: Remember from our earlier discussion that, with the exception of two years in the early '90s, we haven't had tax rates this low in 80 years. This is a window of opportunity that should be taken advantage of before taxes go up for good. Further, we

[20] John T. Adney, "New IRS Letter Ruling Provides Guidance on Substantially Equal Periodic Payments from Immediate Variable Annuities," *Davis & Harman LLP*, September 2008, http://www.davis-harman.com/pub.aspx?ID=VG5wclBRPTO=.

know what tax rates are today. They're a known quantity. Do we pay the taxes now given their historically low levels, or do we roll the dice and hope that sometime down the road our country somehow manages to liquidate trillions of dollars of debt without increasing government revenue? Most would say that a bird in the hand is worth more than two in the bush, so take advantage of historically low tax rates while you still can.

2. **Deductions**: If you're still working, there's a good chance that you have quite a few deductions left. Your house may not be completely paid off, giving you much-needed interest deductions. You may also still have dependents living with you. If your itemized deductions today are substantially higher than your standard deduction and personal exemptions ($20,000 for a married couple), then you'll have the ability to offset a lot of those taxes.

3. **Cash Flow**: If you do utilize the 72(t), you can spend the distributed money on whatever you like. This gives you the option of paying the taxes on the distribution out of the distribution itself. So, for example, if your 72(t) gives you $25,000 per year, your taxes (at 30%) would be $7,500. Pay the taxes out of the $25,000, then shift the remaining $17,500 into your tax-free bucket. This becomes a welcome alternative to those who are younger than 59 ½ who would prefer to do a Roth conversion but who don't have the money in their taxable bucket with which to pay the tax.

Remember, paying taxes is not the end of the world (though some say you can see it from there). What is the end of the world? Having to pay taxes at double the rates at a period in your life when you have very few deductions and can least afford to do so.

For Bob and Sue, I would recommend the 72(t), because it allows them to suppress the growth of those IRAs, mitigating the consequences of having a balance in retirement that's too large. Remember, our goal is to keep their balances small enough that RMDs at 70 ½ can be offset by the standard deduction and personal exemptions.

The amount that they can take out by way of a 72(t) fluctuates based on a number of different factors including the age of the account holder, the age of the beneficiary, and interest rates. A 50-year-old in 2013, for example, can take out about 5% per year. In this case study, I would suggest they do a 72(t) on the full IRA amount. At 5%, they would be required to distribute $25,000 every year for 9 ½ years. Shifting this amount every year will go a long way toward bridling the growth of their IRAs. Remember, we don't want to stop growing their assets, just this particular bucket. Later in this chapter we will discuss how this money should be repositioned.

Recommendation: Shift $25,000 annually
from IRA to tax-free bucket by means of a 72(t).

Taxable Mutual Funds: $100,000

Next, let's address the $100,000 in mutual funds that are serving as the Jones's emergency fund. Using the six-month rule we discussed earlier, we can see that the Joneses have about twice as much money in their emergency funds as is the recommended requirement. If they make $100,000 per year, then six months of income is about $50,000. So, not only do they have too much in their emergency fund, but they are further compounding the problem by growing these dollars in mutual funds. To address this, we must shift both growth and principal on that $100,000 into the tax-free bucket.

Now, before we start shifting money out of the taxable or tax-deferred buckets into tax-free, it's important to keep a few things in mind:

1. You want to shift money out in an incremental stream, *not* all at once.

2. In some cases, you must pay a tax when transferring money into the tax-free bucket. If you shift money out all at once, especially in the case of the tax-deferred bucket, you run the risk of bumping up into a higher tax bracket.

3. Most tax-free investments have limits on how much you can shift in any given year. As you'll recall, the maximum annual contribution to the Roth IRA for two 50-year-olds is $13,000 per year (as of 2013).[21] Even the LIRP ties contribution levels to death benefit amounts. Further, we can only maintain the tax-free status of the LIRP when we stream money into it over a period of time. When we make huge lump sum contributions to the LIRP, we risk turning it into a modified endowment contract (MEC). The cash buildup inside the LIRP would then be re-characterized as tax-deferred and not tax-free.

With these considerations in mind, the Joneses need to find an amount they can shift out of their taxable bucket each and every year so that, by the time they retire in 15 years, they have the ideal emergency fund. What is the ideal balance? In Bob and Sue's case, it's about $50,000 in today's dollars. So, 15 years from now, $50,000 adjusted for 3% inflation is about $78,000. If their mutual funds are growing at an after tax rate of 5% every year, they would need to shift about $5,500 per year for the next 15 years. That would leave their taxable bucket at the $78,000 objective by the time they reach 65.

Recommendation: Shift $5,500 per year
from taxable mutual funds to the tax-free bucket.

401(k): 10% Contributions with No Match

Let me start by reinforcing a ground rule that I laid out earlier. The only time that it makes sense to contribute to a 401(k) is if your employer is giving you free money. We call this a match. It gives you an instant return on your investment. Free money is good! As a reminder, there is an ideal balance to have in the tax-deferred bucket. You can have too much, but you can also have too little. If you have too little money in this bucket,

[21] "Roth IRA Contribution Limits 2013," *Roth IRA Central*, http://roth-ira-contribution-limits.com/roth-ira-contribution-limits-2013.

the best way of growing it is to make contributions up to the match, but not beyond. If you already have a substantial amount of money in your 401(k), additional contributions beyond the match could create a balance that's too large by the time you reach retirement.

Remember, our goal in most cases is to bridle the growth of the tax-deferred bucket. If you're doing a 72(t) on your IRA in an attempt to do so, yet you're putting money hand over fist into your 401(k) with no match, then you have a conflicted investment strategy.

In Bob and Sue's case, they are not getting a match, so I recommend that they recapture all their contributions ($10,000) and shift them to their tax-free bucket. We'll talk about where to put this money in a moment.

*Recommendation: Recapture $10,000 annual
401(k) contribution and shift to the tax-free bucket.*

Term Life Insurance Premiums

Bob and Sue are to be commended for having life insurance. A premature death, especially during their peak earning years, is clearly something that could derail their financial plan. There could, however, be a more cost-efficient way of mitigating this risk while enhancing their ability to contribute to the tax-free bucket. I'll explain how shortly.

*Recommendation: Recapture $2,000 annual
term insurance premiums and shift to the tax-free bucket.*

Long-Term Care Insurance: $4,000 per Year for Joint Coverage

As mentioned earlier, long-term care protection is indispensable to most married couples during retirement. A long-term care event, in many cases, can be more financially devastating than the death of a spouse.

Remember, if one spouse dies, the other spouse inherits all the retirement accounts. If a pension is involved and the survivorship option is elected, the death of the primary spouse ensures that the surviving spouse continues to receive that income into perpetuity. And, in the case of Social Security, the surviving spouse always gets the higher of the two Social Security payments on the death of the spouse.

In the case of a long-term care event, however, the government will force you into "spend down" before stepping in to pick up the tab. In other words, if Bob needs long-term care, all the retirement accounts in his name get earmarked for the long-term care facility. In some cases, these assets can be almost entirely spent down before Medicaid steps in and pays the expense. This deprives the community spouse, Sue, of most of the assets and income that she had been relying upon for a comfortable retirement. She would be allowed to keep her Minimum Monthly Maintenance Needs Allowance (MMMNA), $115,920 of assets, one car, and one home.[22] Is this the type of retirement that she was envisioning?

We know that long-term care is a risk that needs to be mitigated, but what's the most cost-effective way of doing so? Remember, traditional long-term care insurance is expensive, can be hard to qualify for, and is a use-it or lose-it proposition. In other words, you could pay into it for 30 years, die peacefully in your sleep never having used it, and not get any of your money back. This reality can give some people heartburn. They're paying a lot of money for something that they hope to never use.

In Bob and Sue's case, we might recommend recapturing this $4,000 and covering the long-term care risk in a completely different way. Whether we do so or not depends upon Bob and Sue's health, the amount of money that they've already paid into their long-term care insurance, and a number of other variables. Assuming that Bob and Sue meet all of these specifications, we'll divert this $4,000 long-term care

---

[22] "Massachusetts Long Term Care & Medicaid frequently asked questions answered by Attorney Stephanie Konarski," *Stephanie Konarski: Estate and Elder Law*, http://www.massestatelawyer.com/long-term-care-medicaid-faqs-massachusetts.

insurance premium to the tax-free bucket. In the meantime, we'll find a more efficient way of dealing with their long-term care needs.

Recommendation: Recapture $4,000 annual long-term care insurance premium and divert to the tax-free bucket.

In summary, by looking at Bob and Sue's assets and insurance through the prism of tax efficiency, we can identify ways to systematically reposition these dollars into the tax-free bucket. Let's take a look at the total amount of recaptured dollars:

Recaptured Money	
72(t)	$25,000
Taxable Mutual Funds	$5,500
401(k)	$10,000
Term Insurance	$2,000
Long-Term Care Insurance	$4,000
Total	$46,500

Not bad. We've recaptured $46,500 on an annual basis that can now be earmarked for tax-free investing, right? Well, not quite. We don't have all $46,500 to work with because some of these strategies require us to pay tax.

The two primary taxable events are the following:

Tax Consequences	
72(t)	$25,000
Recaptured 401(k) Contributions	$10,000
Total Taxable Events	$35,000
Hypothetical Tax Rate	30%
Total Tax Bill	$10,500

As you can see, this strategy requires Bob and Sue to pay taxes on an additional $35,000 at their highest marginal tax rate. Assuming normal levels of deductions, they'd be paying taxes at the 25% federal rate and 5% for state. At 30%, that's an additional $10,500 of taxes every year until they retire.

Do you think that Bob and Sue have $10,500 just lying around that they would *love* to spend on taxes each and every year? Probably not. And if I recommend that they quit going out to eat, stop going on vacation, and pull back the belt a couple of notches just so they can pay this tax bill, they'll probably stop returning my phone calls. Instead, I must find a way to help them pay that annual bill without modifying their lifestyle.

The best way to accomplish this is to have them pay that tax right out of the $46,500 that we just freed up. That would leave us with $36,000 to shift into the tax-free bucket every year for the next 15 years.

Now that we know how much money we can shift every year ($36,000), the question becomes, how can Bob and Sue invest these dollars so that they will grow in a truly tax-free environment? Further, how do we create multiple streams of tax-free income as part of a balanced strategy that will land the Joneses in the 0% tax bracket in retirement?

Tax-Free Stream #1: Roth IRAs

The first thing that I'd recommend is that Bob and Sue fully fund two Roth IRAs. In 2013, two 50-year-olds can contribute $6,500 per year for a total of $13,000. I love Roth IRAs because they meet both of the attributes required of a truly tax-free investment:

1. **No Taxation:** Distributions from Roth IRAs are free from federal, state, and capital gains tax, so long as you're 59 ½ or over.

2. **No Social Security Tax:** Roth IRA distributions don't count against income thresholds that cause Social Security benefits to be taxed.

By contributing $13,000 to Roth IRAs, we're left with $23,000 that needs to be shifted into the tax-free bucket on an annual basis. But what tax-free vehicle allows us to contribute $23,000 per year?

Tax-Free Stream #2: The LIRP

Remember, the LIRP is a tax-free vehicle that enjoys all of the tax-free qualities of the Roth IRA, without the traditional constraints. Let's briefly summarize the attributes that make the LIRP an effective tax-free accumulation tool:

1. Access to cash value prior to 59 ½ with no penalty
2. Growth of money does not generate a 1099 tax bill
3. Distributions are taken out tax-free regardless of age
4. No contribution limits
5. No income limitations
6. No legislative risk

The attribute that is most relevant to our discussion at this point is #4: No contribution limits. Since we need to find a tax-free home for $23,000 on an annual basis, this attribute becomes essential to our strategy. Given the LIRP's flexible contributions limits, we can now move all $23,000 into the tax-free bucket.

As you'll recall, the LIRP is not just a tax-free accumulation tool, it's also a way to hedge against the risk of premature death. That explains the "Life Insurance" in "Life Insurance Retirement Plan." The IRS allows you to contribute nearly unlimited amounts to the LIRP, as long as you're willing to pay for the cost of term insurance out of these contributions. Imagine a bucket with a spigot attached to the side of it. You shift dollars into the bucket on an annual basis. In the meantime, the cost of term insurance drips out of that spigot.

In our scenario, Bob and Sue have already budgeted $2,000 per year for the cost of term insurance. Instead of sending that $2,000 off to an insurance company in the form of a term insurance premium payment, why not contribute it to the LIRP, let a portion of it drip out of the spigot in the form of expenses, and then avail Bob and Sue of a huge bucket of tax-free dollars that wasn't previously available to them?

Depending upon the insurance company you decide to use, this death benefit can also double as long-term care insurance. Many companies that sponsor LIRPs say that in the event that you can't perform 2 of 6 activities of daily living (such as eating, bathing, dressing, etc.), they will give you a portion of the death benefit while you're alive for the purpose of paying for long-term care.[23] This feature allows us to give Bob and Sue long-term care coverage without the traditional costs of long-term care insurance.

The Jones's Asset Shifting Strategy

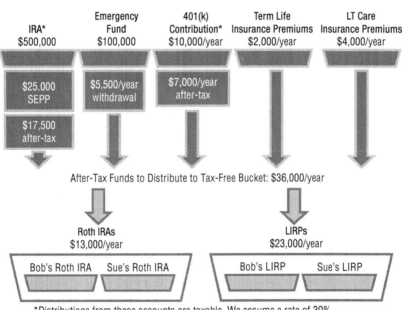

The illustration above demonstrates the asset shifting strategy needed for Bob and Sue's 0% tax bracket strategy.

---

[23] "Long Term Care Insurance Activities of Daily Living Defined," *ExplainMyClaim.com*, http://www.explainmyclaim.com/adls.html.

Because Bob and Sue both have the need for life insurance and long-term care coverage, they'll each need their own separate LIRP. We must divide that $23,000 between their respective LIRPs so that they both have the appropriate level of life insurance and long-term care protection.

Tax-Free Stream #3: A Tax-Free Traditional IRA

That's right, you read it correctly: *Tax-Free* Traditional IRA. *Hold the phone*, you must be thinking. *Surely there's no way to take money out of an IRA tax-free…at least not legally, right?* If you'll recall from our earlier discussions, Bob and Sue will likely be using their standard deduction and personal exemptions in retirement. If they retired today, that would amount to $20,000. Because the IRS has historically adjusted this number to keep up with inflation (3% per year), these deductions will be closer to $30,000 by the time they retire in 15 years at age 65. Because of this, Bob and Sue will be able to take as much as $30,000 out of their IRA without paying any taxes at all.

Because we did the 72(t) on their IRAs, we bridled the growth of these accounts. If we did an exceptionally good job of keeping those accounts from growing, then they would still have $500,000 left in their IRAs at age 65. Bob and Sue could then take distributions out of their IRA up to the level of their deductions ($30,000) without paying a dime in tax.

Remember, had we allowed Bob and Sue to grow this IRA in an unbridled way, it would have been worth somewhere north of $1.5 million by the time they retired. The RMDs on this amount alone would have overwhelmed their standard deductions, at which point they would show up on the IRS's radar. It would then be impossible for them to be in the 0% tax bracket.

By keeping Bob and Sue's IRAs at $500,000, we keep their RMDs below their annual deductions. And, so long as we keep these RMDs below their annual deductions, we preserve the tax-free nature of these assets.

Caveat: Now, just because Bob and Sue can take $30,000 out of their IRAs tax-free, doesn't mean that they should. Remember, any distributions coming out of their IRA will count as provisional income, increasing the likelihood that their Social Security will be taxed. The threshold at which 50% of their Social Security becomes taxable is $32,000. The threshold at which 85% of their Social Security gets taxed is $44,000. The IRS has not traditionally adjusted these thresholds to keep up with inflation (though my fingers are crossed that they will in the future). Unfortunately, half of Bob and Sue's Social Security already counts against this threshold. If their combined Social Security is $30,000, then they've already eaten up $15,000 of that $32,000 amount. To avoid hitting that $32,000 threshold, the maximum they could take out of their IRAs that year is $16,999.

At $31,999 of provisional income, Bob and Sue can still receive their Social Security 100% tax-free.

$$\$15,000 + \$16,999 = \$31,999$$

Tax-Free Stream #4: Social Security

Because Tax-Free Recommendations #1, #2 and #3 either do not count as provisional income or do not exceed the minimum IRS thresholds for provisional income, Bob and Sue's Social Security benefits will not be taxed. Not having your Social Security benefits taxed is one of the single greatest things that could ever happen to your retirement. This fact alone can extend your retirement by five to seven years! Remember, if you *do* have to pay taxes on your Social Security benefits, you'll have to take an additional contribution out of your IRA to compensate for it. If your Social Security benefits are tax-free, not only do you get more money but you extend the life of all your other assets!

In Summary

Once you know the ideal balance to have in the taxable and tax-deferred buckets, you can then reposition any surplus dollars into the tax-free bucket. In Bob and Sue's case, we were able to create four streams of tax-free retirement income, none of which show up on the IRS's radar and all of which contribute to their being in the 0% tax bracket.

1. **Roth IRAs**: tax-free
2. **LIRPs**: tax-free
3. **IRAs**: tax-free

Because the first three streams of income are tax-free and below provisional income thresholds, we can now count on a fourth stream of tax-free income:

4. **Social Security**: tax-free (as long as IRA distributions are below $16,999)

If Bob and Sue have four streams of tax-free income, what tax bracket does that put them in? You guessed it: The 0% tax bracket. So, is it possible to be in the 0% tax bracket in retirement? Not only is it possible, it's crucial to the success of your retirement plan.

Why do I make such a big deal about being in the 0% tax bracket? Because the next best alternative isn't very attractive. Let's say that Bob and Sue only implement half of my recommendations and end up missing the 0% tax bracket. What's the next best tax bracket? It isn't the 1%, 2%, or even 5% bracket. In 2013, the next best tax bracket is 10%. Throw in another 5% for state tax, and you're looking at a best case scenario of losing 15% of your tax-deferred bucket to taxes. And if what David Walker says comes true and taxes have to double just to keep our country solvent, then that 15% becomes 30%. All of a sudden, second place isn't looking all that great.

Diversifying Your Tax-Free Streams of Income

Am I recommending that you put all your eggs in one basket? No, I'm advocating multiple streams of income, none of which show up on the IRS's radar. One of the reasons that we do this is because, at any point, the IRS could legislate any one of your tax-free streams of income right out of existence. By having a combination of tax-free alternatives, you insulate yourself against legislative risk. A well-balanced approach to tax-free retirement planning can rely on as many as six or more different streams of tax-free income. Just as you diversify your investments, you should likewise diversify your tax-free streams of income.

SEVEN

PENSIONS AND THE 0% TAX BRACKET

O ne of the most common questions I hear at the end of a workshop is, "What if I have a pension?" If you do have a pension, the first thing that I recommend is "Don't panic!" Although a pension is generally something you have little or no control over from a taxability standpoint, there is much you can change about the rest of your retirement assets through shifting.

The first thing that you need to do is focus on the assets that *can* be moved into the tax-free bucket. The amount of your investable assets that needs to be repositioned to tax-free depends entirely upon the size of your pension.

If Your Pension Is Less Than Your Standard Deduction and Personal Exemptions…

If your household's combined annual pensions during retirement are less than or equal to your standard deduction plus personal exemptions ($20,000 in 2013 dollars), then it's still possible for you to be in the 0% tax bracket. Your pensions would be offset by these deductions and would therefore not be taxable. For example, if your pension at retirement is projected to be $10,000 per year and your standard deductions and personal exemptions at that point are $30,000 ($20,000 adjusted for inflation over about 15 years), your pension would be tax-free.

In this example, you would still have $20,000 of deductions remaining, which means that you should still have some money in your tax-deferred bucket. The ideal balance would generate an RMD at 70 ½ years old small enough to be offset by your remaining deductions and exemptions ($20,000). At age 70 ½, your RMD is 3.65% of your IRA balances. So, $20,000 represents 3.65% of what number?

In order to arrive at this ideal balance, you would likely have to start shifting some of those tax-deferred dollars into the tax-free bucket today, using either a 72(t) or Roth conversion. By postponing this shift until retirement, you risk tax rates being much higher than they are today. Additionally, you would disqualify yourself from being in the 0% tax bracket during the retirement years when that shifting is taking place. You may also find that you have to shift much larger amounts of money because your assets by that time will have grown and compounded. Further, when you shift assets during retirement, the additional provisional income causes your Social Security to be taxed.

My only caveat is that when you have a pension, it may not always be possible to get your Social Security tax-free. If you are married and your pension in retirement is $20,000 per year and one-half of your Social Security is $15,000, then your total provisional income is $35,000. That's greater than the $32,000 threshold, at which point 50% of your Social Security gets taxed at your highest marginal tax bracket. Just remember, we worry about the things that we can control, not the things that we can't!

If Your Pension Is Greater Than Your Standard Deduction and Personal Exemptions...

If the combined annual pensions in your household are greater than the standard deduction and personal exemptions ($20,000 in 2013 dollars), then we know that it's mathematically impossible to be in the 0% tax bracket. Your deductions will be consumed by your pension and any additional income will, by definition, be taxable. There's just no way around it. That's one of the inherent risks of having a pension in retirement. If you do have a pension of this size, we will focus on the rest of your liquid assets because we still have the ability to affect these assets' taxability in the future.

For starters, if your pension in retirement will be greater than $20,000 in 2013 dollars, the ideal amount of money to have in your tax-deferred bucket is zero. Since your pension and one-half of your Social Security are counted as provisional income, a portion of your Social Security will also be counted as taxable income. This will push you into a higher tax bracket in retirement than you might think.

For example, if your pension is $60,000 per year and your Social Security is $40,000 per year, then your provisional income, at the very least, is $80,000. As a result, 85% of your Social Security now gets counted as taxable income, along with all $60,000 of your pension. Even after a normal amount of deductions, you would still be in the 25% federal tax bracket. This means that anything you distribute from tax-deferred accounts, such as IRAs or 401(k)s, will be taxed right on top of your pension and Social Security. In the best-case scenario, the cost of unlocking those tax-deferred dollars would be 25%.

What does all this mean? It means that if you're currently in a 25% federal tax bracket and still have room before you bump up against the 28% tax bracket, you should strike while the iron's hot. Shift dollars out of your tax-deferred bucket and into the tax-free bucket by way of a Roth conversion or 72(t), depending on your age and ability to pay the tax. You see, if the cost of unlocking your tax-deferred dollars in retirement will never be better than 25%, why wouldn't you take advantage of that tax bracket today? By waiting to unlock those tax-deferred dollars for another 5, 10, or 15 years, you risk losing out on that 25% bracket if tax rates rise dramatically. If you wait until 2020 or beyond to unlock these dollars and your marginal tax bracket is 50%, you may look back on this period of historically low taxes and wish you had taken advantage of tax rates while they were on sale!

To see how this might work in real life, consider the following example. Steve and Jennifer Johnson, both age 55, are looking to retire by 65. Their household taxable income is $80,000, and they think their assets can grow at a net rate of return of 6.5%.

The Johnson's Financial Profile	
Steve's IRA	$300,000
Jennifer's IRA	$100,000
Taxable Mutual Funds	$200,000
Steve's Annual Pension*	$72,000
Steve's Monthly Social Security at Age 65	$2,000
Jennifer's Monthly Social Security at Age 65	$1,000

*with COLA and no lump-sum option

As we consider the Johnsons' case, the first question we must ask is, "Is it possible for them to *ever* be at a 0% tax bracket?" Because Steve must receive his pension as a stream of income (there is no lump-sum option), the 0% tax bracket will be forever out of their reach. Steve's pension of $72,000 will be much greater than his standard deductions and personal exemptions (adjusted for inflation, about $27,000 at age 65), so he will have to be in a tax bracket, and it won't be zero. At the very least, $45,000 of his pension will be taxable ($72,000 of pension minus $27,000 of deductions).

Furthermore, his pension ($72,000) and half of their combined Social Security ($18,000) is counted as provisional income. Since this total ($90,000) surpasses the $44,000 threshold, 85% of Social Security income becomes taxable.

What will the Johnsons' taxable income be *before* taking withdrawals from their IRAs in retirement? Well, 85% of $36,000 (their combined annual Social Security benefits) is $30,600. Add that to Steve's pension of $72,000 and you get $102,600. Subtract $27,000 ($20,000 indexed at 3% per year for 10 years) for standard deduction and personal exemptions, and the Johnsons will be looking at taxable income at age 65 of at least $75,600. At today's tax rates, that would put them in the 25% tax bracket. However, if what David Walker says comes true and tax rates rise dramatically over time, then that 25% becomes a *best-case* scenario.

What's the point of all this extra math? Our additional legwork helped us to determine that the Johnsons' permanent streams of taxable income in retirement will always put them in at least the 25% tax bracket. It's likely to be the lowest tax bracket that they'll experience in their lifetime. Any additional distributions out of their IRAs during retirement will land right on top of all this taxable income and will likewise be taxed at that 25% rate. That's assuming that tax rates don't go up. If tax rates in retirement are likely to be higher than they are today, then the perfect balance in their tax-deferred bucket is zero!

So, what's the solution?

Now that we know that Steve and Jennifer's perfect IRA balance in retirement is zero, they can begin shifting these dollars to the tax-free bucket, taking advantage of low tax rates while they're still around. Let's assume that the Johnsons' taxable income this year is $80,000, putting them at a marginal tax bracket of 25%. As of 2013, the 25% tax bracket maxes out at $146,400. Assuming that tax rates stay level, this means the Johnsons can shift $66,400 per year out of their IRAs into the tax-free bucket. By shifting $66,400 per year, they will have reduced their IRAs to zero by age 63, two years before their planned retirement (assuming asset growth of 6.5% per year).

By beginning the shifting process today, the Johnsons take advantage of our historically low tax rates and get most of the heavy lifting done before tax rates are likely to rise.

Assuming a federal tax rate of 25% and an additional 5% for state, this shifting strategy would incur additional annual taxes of $19,920.

Remember, the Johnsons can't pay that tax out of the IRAs themselves because they would incur a 10% penalty for early withdrawal (remember, they're both 55). But they do have $200,000 in taxable mutual funds and could easily pay that $19,920 tax bill out of that bucket. By doing so, they would be taking their least valuable dollars (taxable) and using them as a catalyst to springboard their second-least valuable dollars (tax-deferred) into their most valuable bucket (tax-free). After paying that $19,920 tax bill out of their taxable bucket, they can now shift all $66,400 into the tax-free bucket.

Before we discuss which combinations of tax-free alternatives will best meet their needs, let me highlight an important aspect of the Johnsons' financial profile. As you can see, most of the Johnsons' major assets are in Steve's name.

It's important to assess who owns which assets because it has major repercussions for long-term care. If Steve were to need long-term care, for example, all the assets in his name would be earmarked for the long-term care facility. The only problem is that Jennifer was planning on using these assets to support her lifestyle in retirement! Now she must try to get by on her IRA ($100,000), her Minimum Monthly Maintenance Needs Allowance (MMMNA), and any money remaining in her taxable mutual funds, up to $115,920.[24]

Should Jennifer need long-term care, only her smaller IRA ($100,000), her Social Security income ($1,000 per month), and a portion of their joint mutual funds (anything above $115,920) would go to the long-term care facility. Once her IRA was consumed, she would then qualify for Medicaid. If that were to happen, Steve could easily survive on his $72,000 pension, his IRA, and the exempted portion of his Social Security. Given this reality, Steve has a glaring need for long-term care protection—much more so than Jennifer.

If that's the case, it could make sense for Steve to divert a portion of the $66,400 annual shift, say $20,000, to a Life Insurance Retirement Plan (LIRP). When structured properly, this could give him all the tax-free

[24] For a reminder of these concepts, see Chapter 5.

growth opportunities available within the Roth IRA while providing a death benefit that could be accelerated for the purpose of paying for long-term care. The remaining $46,400 could then be converted to a Roth IRA on an annual basis.

While it is not possible for the Johnsons to get to the 0% tax bracket because of Steve's pension, we've maximized the tax efficiency of their portfolio by doing the following:

1. We reduced their IRAs to the perfect balance (zero) through asset shifting while taking advantage of historically low tax rates.

2. We utilized their least valuable assets—their taxable mutual funds—as a catalyst to reposition their IRAs into the tax-free bucket.

3. We protected the Johnsons against a long-term care event on Steve by utilizing a LIRP while at the same time accumulating tax-free dollars for retirement.

4. We utilized a Roth conversion to help reposition their IRAs into the tax-free bucket in order to protect against tax-rate risk.

In summary, having a pension is not a good reason to throw in the towel when it comes to protecting yourself against the threat of rising taxes. While it's true that you have no control over your pension's taxation in retirement, there is still a lot you *can* control. By knowing your pension amount in advance, you can determine the right amount of money to have in your tax-deferred bucket. Once that's determined, you can begin a shifting program that will get you as close to the 0% tax bracket as is mathematically possible. Although your pension may always be taxable, you can still be in the 0% bracket as it relates to your other assets. Begin by identifying which shifting needs to take place today and then systematically reposition these dollars into the tax-free bucket *before* tax rates go up. An experienced tax-free retirement specialist can help you navigate the complexities and pitfalls you may encounter during the shifting process.

EIGHT

THE TAX-FREE ROAD MAP

E ven under the "traditional" tax-deferred approach to retirement planning, I'm a big fan of having a financial advisor. The fact is, unless you have an expert to help you manage your road to retirement, emotion can often impede the process and erode rates of return. You've heard the old adage, "buy low and sell high," right? Well, when investors succumb to their emotions, they typically do just the opposite. As an example of this, look at the investor carnage in the wake of the 2008 market crash. I can tell you countless stories of investors who, absent a financial advisor, waited until the market had fallen 50% to 60% before they decided to pull out. Then, having been so traumatized by their losses, they kept their money on the sidelines as the stock market rebounded and returned to its near-2007 highs.

In many cases, this happened simply because there wasn't anyone there to "talk them off the ledge." Study after study shows that emotion-driven investing can erode more growth from your portfolio than almost any other factor.[25,26] For that reason alone, I'm a huge advocate of having someone to hold your hand along the way.

[25] Philip Z. Maymin and Gregg S. Fisher, "Preventing Emotional Investing: An Added Value of an Investment Advisor," *The Journal of Wealth Management* 13, no. 4 (2011).

[26] Brad M. Barber, Yi-Tsung Lee, Yu-Jane Liu, and Terrance Odean, "Just How Much Do Individual Investors Lose By Trading?" AFA 2006 Boston Meetings Paper (May 2007).

Emotion isn't the only thing that can derail your retirement plan, especially when it comes to tax-free retirement planning. As you may have observed, the pursuit of the 0% tax bracket is a bit more involved than traditional tax-deferred investing. It takes a good blueprint, constant course adjustments, and the foresight to anticipate the pitfalls which may arise along the way. In this chapter, we will discuss the value of partnering with a tax-free planning specialist who can assist you in the creation of what I call a "Tax-Free Road Map." This road map can be described as an asset shifting schedule based on your current balances, contributions, and anticipated rates of growth. Having both a tax-free planning specialist and a Tax-Free Road Map is indispensable to helping you navigate the pitfalls along your way to the 0% tax bracket.

Finding the Perfect Balance in Each Bucket

One of the recurring themes in this book has been the importance of accumulating the right amount of money in each of the three buckets. Having the wrong balance in any of these accounts can have massive unintended consequences for you in your pursuit of the 0% tax bracket.

The Taxable Bucket

Determining the ideal balance in the taxable bucket is the first step. In Chapter 2, we established that the perfect balance is the amount necessary to safeguard against life's unexpected emergencies—about six months' worth of income. While this seems straightforward enough, difficulties arise if you have too much money in this bucket and need to reposition it to the tax-free bucket. Let's say, for example, that your ideal balance is $50,000 yet you have accumulated $200,000. To compound the problem, you have it in mutual funds and it's growing at 5% per year. Remember, you can't shift the entire $150,000 surplus into the tax-free bucket all in one year. Due to the contribution limitations of the various tax-free alternatives we've covered, your money has to be shifted over a period of time. But how much should you shift each year, over how many years, and into which tax-free accounts? The answers to all these questions can be found in the creation of a Tax-Free Road Map.

The Tax-Deferred Bucket

The real complexity emerges, however, when trying to determine the ideal balance in the tax-deferred bucket. As previously mentioned, when you fail to temper the growth of this bucket, it can be nearly impossible to be in the 0% tax bracket in retirement. On the other hand, when you do not have enough money in this bucket, you won't be able to fully utilize your standard deductions and personal exemptions in retirement. This means that you may have unwittingly shifted too much money into the tax-free bucket, paying unnecessary taxes along the way.

When a tax-free planning specialist is building your Tax-Free Road Map, he will consider a number of variables in determining the ideal balance in this account. What will your standard deduction and personal exemptions be in the year you retire? Are you contributing to your retirement plan above and beyond the match? If so, to what extent? What are your projected rates of return? Do you have a pension? If so, will it be more or less than your anticipated deductions and personal exemptions? Does it have a cost-of-living adjustment (COLA)? Should you do a 72(t) or a Roth conversion?

As I mentioned in Chapter 4, the speed with which you shift these dollars matters. You want to shift dollars slowly enough that you don't inadvertently bump into a higher tax bracket, but quickly enough that you get all the heavy lifting done before tax rates go up. This is where a Tax-Free Road Map is indispensable. An experienced tax-free planning specialist can process all the variables unique to your situation and then determine the exact amounts that should be shifted annually to each of the tax-free alternatives.

The Tax-Free Bucket

Any dollars above and beyond the ideal balance in the first two buckets should be systematically redirected to the tax-free bucket. Any surplus contributions should likewise be redirected toward tax-free alternatives. A properly designed Tax-Free Road Map will incorporate the tax-free alternatives that will best meet your needs. Does a Roth IRA make sense? Do income thresholds require you to use a nondeductible IRA and then convert to Roth? Do your other IRA balances preclude you from using the nondeductible IRA conversion strategy? What about a LIRP? How can this best be utilized to meet your tax-free retirement, life insurance, and long-term care needs? How do you structure the LIRP to maximize returns within the tax-free growth account?

A properly designed Tax-Free Road Map can also help transform your Social Security from a highly taxable stream of income into one that remains tax-free throughout your retirement. As a reminder, having your Social Security get taxed in retirement can be financially devastating. By losing a portion of your Social Security to taxes, you must compensate by taking additional distributions from your other investments. This act alone can deplete your assets five to seven years faster than not having your Social Security taxed at all.

But making sure your Social Security is tax-free requires a tricky balance. You want to take tax-free distributions out of your tax-deferred bucket (up to your standard deductions and personal exemptions), but only to the extent that it does not breach the thresholds that cause your Social Security to get taxed.

Your Tax-Free Road Map can help you balance all these competing interests and ensure that the pursuit of one goal doesn't impact the pursuit of another. Meeting with your tax-free planning specialist at least annually will help you navigate the pitfalls of the tax-deferred bucket and ensure the proper balances at retirement.

The LIRP

Utilizing the LIRP in a thoughtful, well-balanced approach to tax-free retirement involves evaluating a number of different factors. The most important decision happens at the outset when you determine how to best grow the dollars within your LIRP's growth account. If you'll recall from Chapter 5, there are three basic options:

1. General Account of the Life Insurance Company
2. The Stock Market
3. An Indexed-based Approach

Once you determine the option that best aligns with your retirement needs, you must then find a company to partner with.

As with anything in life, not all LIRPs are created equal. There are over 300 different companies that offer LIRPs, not all of which are ideal partners in the tax-free retirement process. Your tax-free retirement specialist can assist you in sorting through all the carriers to find the one that will best meet your specific retirement needs. In evaluating these companies, you and your advisor will need to consider the following attributes:

1. **Low expenses**: Whatever drips out of your bucket in the form of expenses won't help you. Not only do you lose those dollars, but you lose the ability to earn interest on them as well. Not all companies' expenses are the same.

2. **Long-term care provisions**: Not all LIRP carriers offer a long-term care provision. Some companies offer them but charge exorbitant fees. If you're looking to mitigate a long-term care risk without having to pay for traditional long-term care insurance, make sure that your LIRP has this important feature.

3. **Cost-free distributions**: All LIRPs give you the ability to take money out tax-free. But not all of them give you the ability to take it out cost-free as well. In fact, some companies charge a rate of interest which, if not repaid, gets deducted from your growth account. So it's critical that you find a company that gives you the ability to take dollars out tax-free and cost-free.

4. **Financial stability:** You could find a company whose LIRP has all the above-mentioned qualities, but unless they're financially stable, you risk foiling your entire plan. Financial stability should be paramount when considering a LIRP company to partner with.

When utilized properly, the LIRP can be a critical cog in your efforts to reach the 0% tax bracket. Finding a company that has a LIRP that aligns with your growth objectives, while also conforming to the above standards can be a tricky proposition. A qualified tax-free retirement specialist understands the LIRP marketplace and can help you navigate all of the various alternatives.

After you've found the right company and chosen the method of growth that best suits your needs, you can then address the structuring of your LIRP. To maximize the returns within your growth account, you must buy as little insurance as is required by the IRS. You must then contribute as much money as is allowed under the IRS guidelines. This strategy ensures that the expenses dripping out of your bucket will be small relative to the money accumulating inside your bucket. Remember, when properly structured, these expenses should average about 1.5% of your bucket per year over the life of the program. A qualified tax-free planning specialist understands how to structure your LIRP and how to incorporate it into your strategy to get to the 0% tax bracket.

Finding a Tax-Free Planning Specialist

As already mentioned, it's difficult, if not impossible, to create a Tax-Free Road Map without the help of someone who's been down this road before. A qualified tax-free planning specialist has the experience and know-how that sets him apart from an ordinary financial advisor. Most traditional financial advisors are mired down in the tax-deferred approach to retirement planning: "You're earning x, I think I can get you x+1." In order to create a Tax-Free Road Map, an advisor must be familiar with all the pitfalls of the traditional tax-deferred investing paradigm and be well-versed in the tax-free strategies that will land you at the 0% tax bracket before tax rates go up for good.

Begin your search by having a discussion with the advisor who gave you this book. If he gave it to you, it's because he felt like it was critical to your financial well-being. This act alone should set this advisor apart from other financial advisors in the world of traditional tax-deferred investing. Begin by asking questions about how these principles apply to your specific situation. If the advisor answers your questions to your satisfaction, proceed to the next step—the creation of a Tax-Free Road Map. Once this road map is complete, you can begin your journey toward the 0% tax bracket!

The graphic below can help you visualize the overall process of executing your tax-free retirement strategy, including the transfer of surplus assets from the taxable and tax-deferred buckets to the tax-free bucket.

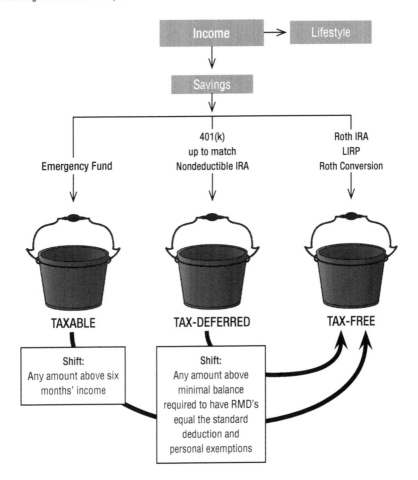

NINE

Frequently Asked Questions

M y main reason for writing this book is to help you understand how to insulate and protect your hard-earned assets from the impact of the tax "freight train" of which I spoke in the first chapter. As I've said throughout the book, the best way to do so is to re-arrange your assets so that you are in the 0% tax bracket when you retire. While the benefits of achieving the 0% tax bracket seem straightforward, the path along the way can be fraught with hazards, pitfalls and unexpected detours. Because of that, I have included this final chapter in an attempt to answer the most commonly asked questions that arise during the planning process. Ultimately, the best way to answer questions that pertain to your specific situation is to consult with a tax-free planning specialist.

General Questions

Q: Am I too old to adopt this strategy?
A: Allow me to answer this question with a few questions of my own. What if you decide not to take advantage of today's historically low tax

rates and postpone the payment of those taxes until a later date? What if at that later date, tax rates are twice as high as they are today? Will you look back at this period of historically low tax rates and say, "Why didn't I take advantage of those rates while they were on sale?" So the real question that you have to consider is this: Do you think you'll still be alive when tax rates are higher than they are today? If so, you're not too old to take advantage of these strategies.

Q: Can I be in the 0% tax bracket and still be a good citizen?

A: Let me answer this by deferring to Judge Learned Hand, the most famous judge that never became a Supreme Court Justice:

"Any one may so arrange his affairs that his taxes shall be as low as possible; he is not bound to choose that pattern which best pays the Treasury; there is not even a patriotic duty to increase one's taxes."[27]

"Over and over again the courts have said that there is nothing sinister in so arranging one's affairs as to keep taxes as low as possible. Everybody does so, rich or poor; and all do right, for nobody owes any public duty to pay more than the law demands."[28]

I would like to emphasize one additional point. We're not suggesting that you not pay taxes. The cost of getting into the tax-free bucket is that you have to be willing to pay taxes today. We're simply suggesting that you pay taxes at historically low tax rates to avoid potentially higher rates later on.

Q: If this is so great, why isn't everyone doing it?

A: I've found that many advisors who adhere to the traditional tax-deferred approach to retirement planning can be averse to this type of planning. Here's why: The typical financial planner makes a living by managing your money. A typical fee might be 1% of your assets per year. If a financial advisor is managing your $1,000,000 IRA, then he's making about $10,000 per year. If he convinces you that taxes in the future are

---

[27] *Gregory v. Helvering*, 69 F.2d 809, 810 (2d Cir. 1934).
[28] *Commissioner v. Newman*, 159 F.2d 848, 851 (2d Cir. 1947).

going to be substantially higher than today, you might feel compelled to shift that $1,000,000 into the tax-free bucket. The problem is, the tax-free bucket has a cost of admission: taxes. Let's say that you pay 30% in taxes to get into the tax-free bucket. Your advisor is now only managing $700,000 of your money. If he's still making 1% of your total assets, he just cut his pay from $10,000 to $7,000. Most financial advisors get paid to make your money grow, not to maximize your distributions in retirement. It is important that your money grow in retirement, but it's critical that it grow in the right environment. Remember, not all buckets are created equal.

Questions about the Taxable Bucket

Q: What happens if I receive an inheritance?

A: One of the most important questions that we can ask in the planning process is the timing and amount of inheritances. You see, most inheritances come to you in the form of a check, which you promptly deposit into your checking account (i.e., the taxable bucket). You could have spent ten years shifting assets out of your taxable bucket into the tax-free bucket, only to see your prospects of getting to the 0% tax bracket dashed by this unexpected windfall. For that purpose, it's important to try to guesstimate the timing and amounts of inheritance (as hard as that is to do) so that your Tax-Free Road Map can make provisions for that money to be shifted into the tax-free bucket.

Q: What if I want to have more than six months' worth of income in my taxable bucket?

A: It's acceptable to have more than six months' worth of income in this bucket so long as you recognize that it comes at a price. Since a disproportionate percentage of your net worth is taxable, you could end up paying more taxes than is necessary and, ultimately, risk having a portion of your Social Security taxed.

Questions about the Tax-Deferred Bucket

Q: Is there ever an instance where I would not want to contribute to my 401(k) up to my employer's match?

A: Actually there is. Remember, one of the main goals of your Tax-Free Road Map should be to make your Social Security tax-free, if possible. In some cases, making a contribution to your 401(k) just so that you can get an anemic match could ultimately cause your Social Security to be taxed.

For example, your 401(k) requires you to contribute 6% of your income in order to get a 25-cents-on-the-dollar match. You're deferring a significant portion of your income to your 401(k) just so that you can capture this infinitesimally small match. As a result, you're pumping up your 401(k) to the point where your RMDs may be so large that your Social Security becomes taxed. It might make more sense to forgo the match and divert that 6% to your tax-free bucket to increase the likelihood of getting your Social Security tax-free. Once again, a tax-free planning specialist can help you understand if your 401(k)'s match is big enough to justify making a contribution.

Questions about the Roth IRA

Q: Can the government decide to tax your Roth IRA at retirement?

A: Since 1997, the IRS has given you the option of being taxed on the "seed" or on the "harvest." With a Roth IRA, you're taxed on the seed; with a traditional IRA, you're taxed on the harvest. To tax you on both the seed and the harvest would be unprecedented and would likely get more than a few politicians thrown out of office. A more likely scenario would be for the IRS to eliminate all future contributions to the Roth IRA. You'd likely keep what was in there, but lose the ability to make further contributions.

Q: What is the 5-year rule with the Roth IRA?

A: This rule determines whether or not distributions from your Roth IRA are taxable. First of all, all contributions can be taken from your Roth IRA at any time without tax and without penalty. In order to take the growth out of these accounts penalty-free, you have to be at least 59 ½ and have had an established Roth IRA account for at least five years. For example, let's say that you're 60 and you make a first-time contribution of $6,500 to a Roth IRA that grows to $7,000 by the time you're 61. You could withdraw the $6,500 at any point, but would have to wait until five years after your initial contribution date to access the growth. The initial contribution date is January 1st of the tax year in which you made the contribution.

Q: If I'm working part time in retirement, can I still contribute to a Roth IRA?

A: To contribute to a Roth IRA, you have to have earned income—you have to be earning a paycheck. For anyone over age 50, you can contribute whatever your earned income is or $6,500 (in 2013), whichever is less. If you and your spouse are over 50 and only one of you is working, you can contribute up to $13,000 or whatever your earned income is, whichever is less.

Questions about Roth Conversions

Q: What is the 5-year rule with the Roth conversion?

A: If you do a Roth conversion before you are 59 ½, you have to wait five years or until 59 ½, whichever comes first, before you can touch the principal without tax and penalty. If you're already 59 ½ when you make the conversion, you can touch the principal immediately but have to wait five years before you touch any of the earnings without penalty.

Q: Does the Roth conversion have income limitations?

A: Prior to 2010, there was a $100,000 income limitation, but now anyone can do a Roth conversion regardless of income level.

Q: How quickly should I convert my Roth IRA?

A: Quickly enough that you pay the taxes owed before tax rates rise dramatically, but slowly enough that you don't bump yourself into a dramatically higher tax bracket.

Q: Does it ever make sense to convert my IRA to a Roth all in one year?

A: The first scenario in which you might want to convert all of your IRA in one year is if it's small enough to keep you in a reasonably low tax bracket. For example, if you make $100,000 per year and you have a $30,000 IRA, you could convert all of it while staying in the 25% tax bracket.

The second scenario in which it might make sense to convert all of your IRA to a Roth in one year is if you anticipate always being in the highest marginal tax bracket. For example, if you're currently in the highest marginal tax bracket (39.6% today) and don't see that changing in retirement, you could convert unlimited amounts of IRAs and only be taxed at 39.6%. This especially makes sense if you think the highest marginal tax rate in the future will rise over time. Take advantage of the low rates today and get all the shifting done in one year.

Questions about the LIRP

Q: What are the expenses in the LIRP?

A: Most LIRPs have some administrative expenses, but the majority of expenses come from the cost of insurance. These expenses are greater in the early years and lower in the later years. But, considered over the life of the program, they should end up costing you about 1.5% of your bucket per year, assuming the policy is structured to maximize cash accumulation. This is very similar to the expenses that you might find in a traditional 401(k). In the 401(k), you're paying three different people or entities—the money manager, the financial advisor, and the third-party administrator. In the LIRP, you don't pay these expenses, but you do pay the cost of insurance. The difference with the LIRP is that the 1.5% you pay per year over the life of the program actually gets you a real, substantive benefit, which you can then utilize during your lifetime for the purpose of long-term care or at death as a death benefit.

Q: How soon can I touch my money?

A: LIRPs generally have a surrender period or vesting schedule, similar to a 401(k). These restrictions exist because life insurance companies incur substantial expenses when getting these programs up and running. By putting a surrender period in place, they're simply saying that, should you decide to cash everything in and run for the border, they reserve the right to recuperate all those expenses they incurred at the outset of the program. In other words, they don't want to take a bath if you have second thoughts three years into the program. In fact, most of these companies don't manage to break even until seven years into the contract. Having said that, with most LIRPs, you do typically have limited access to the money in the first or second year.

Although it's important to understand what escape hatches you have, you must also bear in mind that this bucket works the best when you allow it to grow and marinate over time. As a general rule, your tax-free vehicles are your most valuable and should be the last to be liquidated in the event of an emergency. Ideally, you want to postpone distributions from these assets until a period of much higher tax rates. Conversely, the best time to shift or spend dollars from tax-deferred assets is during periods of historically low tax rates. By following these rules, you will ultimately have math on your side and be able to wring the most efficiency out of your retirement dollars.

Q: What happens if I run out of money in my LIRP before I die?

A: We want to avoid this scenario at all costs. If you don't have at least $1 in your LIRP at death, the government says that your intent wasn't really to utilize this vehicle as a life insurance contract. So, all the taxes that you avoided along the way would come due all in one year. For that reason, your LIRP must have features that safeguard against this ever happening. Some companies call this provision an over-loan protection rider.

Q: How can distributions from a LIRP be tax-free?

A: Distributions are only tax-free if the money is taken out the correct way. If you take a normal distribution, like you might with a 401(k) or IRA, the money can be taxable. By taking money out by way of a loan, however, then it is tax-free. Any time you receive a loan, whether from the bank or your rich uncle, that money does not show up on your tax return as income. Why? Because the IRS anticipates that you will pay the money back with dollars that have been taxed.

When you take money out of your LIRP, the life insurance company is actually giving you a loan from their own coffers. This is how it works: You call up and say, "I need $10,000." They take $10,000 out of your growth account (with a balance of $100,000) and put it into a loan collateral account that earns 3% per year. Now you have $90,000 in your bucket, right? Wrong. Since you still have $10,000 in your loan collateral account, your bucket technically still contains $100,000.

In the very same transaction, the life insurance company sends you a loan from their own coffers. For this loan, they charge you 3% interest. Remember, loans don't show up on your tax return. When you die, all the money in the loan collateral account is used to pay back the outstanding loan that you have with the company. Because the interest charged on the loan is the same as the interest being credited in the loan collateral account, the net cost to you over the course of your lifetime is zero. In short, you asked for $10,000, you received $10,000 in the mail, your growth account went down by $10,000, and you never paid any tax. That's how we utilize this bucket to take tax-free distributions.

Q: How soon can I take the 0% loan?

A: It depends on the company, but, in some cases, it can be as early as the 1st day of the 6th year.

Q: What if I want to take money out before the 0% loan option is available?

A: As a rule of thumb, if you need to take money out before the 0% loan is available, you can simply take a withdrawal. Any dollars that you've contributed to the program (your basis) can be distributed tax-free as a return on your principal.

Q: What's the difference between death benefit options in a LIRP?

A: You can structure your LIRP's death benefit in two different ways, or "options." With Option 1, as the cash in your account grows, the amount of life insurance that the government requires you to maintain goes down. It follows this formula:

$$\text{Cash Value + Life Insurance = Death Benefit}$$

Let's say that in Day 1 of the program, your cash value is 0. Following the above formula, if your death benefit is $500,000, then the amount of life insurance you're paying for that year is also $500,000. However, 10 years into the program, you might have closer to $100,000 in your growth account. Following that same formula, the amount of life insurance you would pay for that year would only be $400,000.

With Option 2, the amount of life insurance that you're paying for never changes. Therefore, in the above example, if you had cash value of $100,000, then the amount of life insurance you'd be paying for in year 10 would still be $500,000, making your overall death benefit $600,000. For this reason, Option 2 is also referred to as an "Increasing Death Benefit" option.

Q: What limits do I have on how much money I can put into the LIRP?

A: The IRS links contribution levels in the LIRP to death benefit amounts. The greater the death benefit, the more you can contribute. But it's the life insurance companies, not the IRS, that place limits on how much of a death benefit you can have. In the post–9/11 world, this death benefit amount tops out at about 25 times your annual salary, with slight modifications for age. Let's say that you're 45 and make $100,000 per year. Based on the parameters that I just mentioned, the life insurance company would typically allow a death benefit as high as $2,500,000. In this scenario, you would be allowed to contribute up to $170,000 per year!

For all intents and purposes, there are no contribution limits to the LIRP, so long as your death benefit remains at 25 times your salary or less.

Q: What if I run across hard times and can't fund my LIRP for a while?
A: So long as there is money in your surrender value to sustain the expenses that drip out of the spigot, you can stop your contributions.

Q: If I get a big bonus from work, can I just drop it into my LIRP?
A: You can, but it may inhibit you from putting more money in later down the road. Generally, based on the death benefit of your LIRP, there is a finite amount of money that you can contribute over your lifetime. The IRS also requires that you stream this money in over a period of years as opposed to contributing it all in a single year. If you put too much money in during any given year, you can violate the IRS guidelines and lose the tax-free protection of the bucket.

Q: Will the IRS ever change the rules on this program?
A: Most likely yes. As our country slides slowly into insolvency, they'll start looking in all quarters for additional revenue. This program costs the government about $80 billion per year, so they will most likely attempt to eliminate it somewhere in the future. However, if history serves as a model, this program will likely enjoy significant protection from legislative risk. In 1982, 1984, and 1988, the government changed the rules on the LIRP and, when they did, they stipulated that the people who had these programs before the rules changed were allowed to keep them and could continue to contribute to them under the old rule for the rest of their lives. We call this a "grandfather" clause.

Q: Why does the IRS allow a 0% loan?
A: Technically, it's not a 0% loan. You are actually taking a real loan from the life insurance company and being charged a real rate of interest in order to preserve what the IRS calls an "arm's length transaction." The IRS's chief concern is that the life insurance companies charge a

reasonable interest rate. They don't care what the life insurance companies do with the loan collateral account on the other side of the ledger. Some life insurance companies credit back the same exact amount that's being charged in order to make it both a tax-free and cost-free transaction.

Q: How does the long-term care rider work?

A: If you can find a doctor who will write a letter that says you can't perform two of the six activities of daily living (e.g., feeding yourself, bathing yourself, etc.), then some companies will give you your death benefit in advance of your death. Put differently, they will give you your death benefit while you are still alive for the purpose of paying for long-term care. If your death benefit is $300,000, for example, certain companies will send you a check for as much as 2% of that amount, or $6,000 per month, every month for the next 48 months. Whatever portion of the death benefit that doesn't get spent on long-term care will go to your heirs at death.

Q: How do I know that the company who holds my LIRP is going to continue existing in the future?

A: You don't, which is why it's so important to look at a company's financial ratings. This is the best barometer of the financial solvency of a life insurance company.

For additional information on these topics, please visit my website at
www.thepowerofzeropercent.com

ABOUT THE AUTHOR

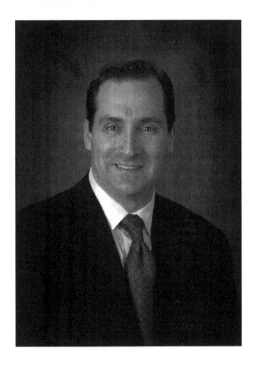

David McKnight graduated from Brigham Young University with Honors in 1997. He is a nationally recognized speaker and his popular workshop, "The Power of Zero," has been seen by thousands of Americans from coast to coast. This workshop was recently showcased at Forum 400, an annual gathering of the top 1% of financial advisors in the nation. In 2014, David will be a Focus Speaker at the worldwide annual conference for Million Dollar Round Table in Toronto, Canada.

David has trained thousands of advisors on the power of the zero percent tax bracket and currently serves as mentor to an exclusive group of financial advisors from across the country. He is the president of David McKnight & Company located in Mequon, Wisconsin.

David is very involved with his family, church, and community. He currently resides in Grafton, Wisconsin, with his wife, Felice, and their six children.